RUDELY STAMP'D
Imaginal Disability and Prejudice

Douglas Biklen
and
Lee Bailey
Editors

Copyright © 1981 by

University Press of America, Inc.

P.O. Box 19101, Washington, D.C. 20036

Printed in the United States of America

ISBN (Perfect): 0-8191-1983-0
ISBN   (Cloth): 0-8191-1982-2

Library of Congress Catalog Card Number: **81-40298**

RUDELY STAMP'D
Imaginal Disability and Prejudice

CONTENTS

CONTRIBUTORS

Douglas Biklen: Division of Special Education & Rehabilitation, Syracuse University

Sidney Thomas: Department of Fine Arts, Syracuse University

John Diehl: Department of English, Syracuse University

Bruce Dearing: Upstate Medical Center, Syracuse, NY

Leonard Kriegel: Department of English, City College of New York

Seymour Sarason: Department of Psychology, Yale University

Lee Bailey: Humanities Ph.D. Program, Syracuse University

INTRODUCTION

When Shakespeare characterized his Richard III as a "rudely stamp'd" villain, he made a notable contribution to the imaginal world of shadowy fantasies of disability:

> But I, that am not shap'd for sportive tricks,
> Nor made to court an amourous looking-glass;
> I, that am *rudely stamp'd* and want love's majesty
> To strut before a wanton ambling nympth;
> I, that am curtail'd of this fair proportion,
> Cheated of feature by dissembling nature,
> Deform'd, unfinish'd, sent before my time
> Into this breathing world, scarce half made up,
> And that so lamely and unfashionable
> That dogs bark at me as I halt by them;
> ...
> since I cannot prove a lover
> To entertain these fair well-spoken days,
> I am determined to prove a villain.
> *(Act I, Scene I)*

Bitter at his imagined love-repelling features, Richard is painted as turning to hateful plots for revenge on his fate.

The thesis of this book is that images such as Richard's in literature and visual art leave numerous individuals who *happen* to have disabilities "rudely stamp'd." To the extent that artistic images of disability influence attitudes, behavior and public policy, disabled people are rudely stamp'd by the shadowy fantasies of the imaginal world. The preconceptions, stereotypes and prejudices reinforced by literary images are the unconscious guides being sought in this book. For to people with disabilities, the burden of this tradition may be far greater than that of biological fate. To a man who happens to be blind or a woman who happens to be deaf, the outrageous rudeness of potentially being stamped as less than they *can* be is borne in the very heart of much literature and visual art. So the task of identifying these unfair preconceptions, unconsciously cultivated in art, has motivated this book.

The *fallacy* we want to call into question is that it is "dissembling nature" whose rude stamp is the only cause for ill treatment of people with disabilities. On the contrary, our research shows how pervasive and unrecognized are the images of disabled characters as helpless or sinister. The task, then, is to demonstrate the extent to which imaginal pictures of disability become thoughtlessly transferred into stereotypical expectations of particular people.

The root problem of disability prejudice is not "dissembling nature" but the images "rudely stamp'd" into the collective, unconscious shadow-world of society. To people with disabilities these fantasies of disability as a horror-show are more than rude, they are unjust and oppressive. Persistently being rudely stamp'd via literature, art and the popular media is an intolerable burden. And the first step in undermining this influence on those who take images literally is to identify these images.

Some of the research in this book focuses on this preliminary task of identifying the images so rudely stamp'd and their imaginal implications. Some research reflects on the sociological matrix: the impact of such images in the family, the media or institutions. Some work raises theoretical questions regarding the origin of stereotypical images. All our efforts strive toward a goal of any liberal education: freedom from oppressive unconscious preconceptions, those "rudely stamp'd" images of fear and delight.

This book was made possible by the Center on Human Policy of Syracuse University, whose staff has spent the last several years in a variety of social change-related activities. We have organized lawsuits on behalf of disabled children who had been denied an education. We have produced exposes of terrible institutional conditions experienced by thousands of retarded people. We have created coalitions of disabled adults, parents of disabled children, and interested citizens to fight for an end to what we have termed handicapist policies and practices. And we have trained hundreds of our students in the purposes and techniques of disability-rights advocacy. Yet we have always been painfully aware that the injustices we fight are rooted in every aspect of our society, and not only in its public policies.

Before we ever thought about producing a book on the subject, we organized a few seminars in which we began to look at the images of people with disabilities in literature, art and film. Two of the first characters to come to mind were Captain Hook and Dr. Strangelove, two disabled villains representative of one kind of stereotypical portrayal. So we entitled our seminars "Captain Hook Meets Dr. Strangelove." The more we examined such imagery, the more convinced we were that this general topic deserved more careful review. This book gathers together several of the papers from these seminars. This interdisciplinary work has flung together scholars from both the social sciences and the humanities with varying theoretical backgrounds. Each has a unique contribution to make to the task of un-concealing those "rudely stamp'd" roots of prejudice.

In various articles, we discover the analogy of the disability rights movement to the struggle against racism and the oppression of women. We recognize the emphasis on the social determinations of illness and disability. We see the impact of a retarded child on a family. We face the multitudes of stereotypes and prejudices bred in art and literature, from disability as something sinister and violent to something incompetent and helpless. We also discover that art and literature can provide us with sentimental defenses against disability, mirrors of our spiritual ugliness, barriers to respect and dignity. We see how disability can provoke the collapse of a family founded on shallow values or stimulate heroic, defiant struggle. We realize that we all must face the cripple in our souls, and stop imagining it to be located in others. And we feel how obsessed our culture is with denying and repressing differences, the passage of time, aging and death.

The articles which comprise this book are merely a beginning. For the problem of the impact of images of disability on prejudice must lead finally to a re-imagining, a re-visioning of both the socio-political and the imaginal* reality so "rudely stamp'd."

Douglas Biklen
Lee Bailey
The Center on Human Policy
Syracuse University
Syracuse, New York
September, 1981

*Note: Our use of the term "imaginal" here is adopted from the French scholar Henri Corbin. He coined the word to imply that works of imagination do not restrict themselves to the irrelevant "imaginary" periphery of consciousness and social policies, but that imagination is inseparable from learning and action. *"Mundis Imaginalis,* or the Imaginary and the Imaginal," *Spring* 1972, 1-19.

SHOULD "THE UGLY DUCKLING" BE BANNED?
by Douglas Biklen

"'Peep,' said the young one, and out he tumbled, but he was so big and ugly." The ugly duckling was born. Immediately, he became the object of verbal assaults, violent attacks, and much conversation. "Things went from bad to worse. The poor duckling was chased and buffeted about by everyone. Even his own brothers and sisters abused him. 'Oh,' they would always say, 'how we wish the cat would catch you, you ugly thing.' And his mother said, 'How I do wish you were miles away.' The ducks nipped him, and the hens pecked him, and the girl who fed them kicked him with her foot." When the wild ducks of the marshes saw him, they told him, "You are terribly ugly, but that's nothing to us so long as you don't marry into our family.'" And so it went until the ugly duckling found others like himself. "What did he see there, mirrored in the clear stream? He beheld his own image, and it was no longer the reflection of a clumsy, dirty, gray bird, ugly and offensive. He himself was a swan!" Indeed, some children who came to feed the group of swans which he had just at this moment joined declared him the youngest and most handsome of all. But he was not proud. "A good heart never grows proud." He remembered all that he had been subject to and mused, 'I never dreamed there could be so much happiness, when I was the ugly duckling!'"

We tend to remember the transformation from ugly duckling to beautiful swan as Hans Christian Anderson's overriding message. Beauty is in the eye of the beholder. It is a moral that most people would embrace, at least in theory. But does not "The Ugly Duckling" bear another message for the reader, perhaps one unintended by Anderson? What if the ugly duckling had *not* become a swan? What if he grew into, simply, a duck which others perceived as ugly? Do we not learn from this story that if one is perceived as ugly, one will be persecuted and scorned? Is it not also apparent that one should pity the ugly duckling for his initial seeming ugliness and for the way others treat him? Perhaps one cannot answer these questions unequivocally. While certain lines, such as the wild ducks' remark that it is all right to be ugly, but "don't marry into our family" are obviously offered as satire, the transformation from duck to swan poses a question as much as it provides an answer. Who can be certain whether the tale suggests that "everyone is beautiful in his or her own way" or whether, instead, that those who conform to a group are beautiful? This latter possibility recalls the earlier questions. What if you are an ugly duckling? What if you do not fit? What if others perceive you as different? Are you condemned to be chased and buffeted about? Will your own family wish you were "miles away?"

Should "The Ugly Duckling" be banned? No. But it should be read or taught with an eye to what it implies about people who are perceived as different. The purpose of this article, and of this book, is to explore the ways in which cultural media create or describe society's treatment of differences. Only by applying a critical perspective to literature, film, news accounts, and a variety of other media, can scholars, writers, teachers and policy makers become more conscious of their own work and its relation to the best interests of people who have disabilities. Viewed anew, stories like "The Ugly Duckling," which once may have seemed so clear in their moral messages, become enigmatic. And some may appear unquestionably prejudicial toward particular groups. Our purpose here is to examine stereotypic and prejudicial, as well as humanistic, attitudes toward disabilities as they appear in cultural media.

The roots of discrimination are found in every area of our personal and social lives, not simply in public laws and policies. Here, we are concerned with media, for the media must be included as part of these roots. Whether the media, used broadly to include everything in literature and film to comic books, newscolumns, and television, create stereotypes and prejudices or simply purvey them, matters little: it only matters that media, like public policy, can either support or discourage stereotypes and prejudices.

We are faced with diverse images indeed. On the one hand there is the "adorable," bumbling Mr. Magoo, a kind of blind Step and Fetchit. On the other is McMurphy in Ken Kesey's *One Flew Over the Cuckoo's Nest,* a strong-willed, humorous and certainly sane man destroyed by insane social structures masquerading as therapies. These are but two of numerous, often contradictory images portrayed through cultural media.

Consider the range of media in which disabled people have played important, if sometimes stereotyped roles. In children's classic stories and fairy tales, there are Captain Hook in J.M. Barrie's *Peter Pan,* Tiny Tim in Dickens' *A Christmas Carol,* the dwarfs in the Grimm's "Snow White and the Seven Dwarfs," the Prince in Mulock's "The Little Lame Prince," Lorenzini's *Pinocchio,* Heidi's crippled friend Clara, Rumplestiltskin and various dwarfs, "hags" and one-legged characters in countless other stories.

In adult literature, there are Quasimodo in Victor Hugo's *The Hunchback of Notre Dame,* Ahab in Melville's *Moby Dick,* the Idiot in Dostoyevski's *The Idiot,* Richard III in Shakespeare's *King Richard III* and, more recently, Philip Carey in Maugham's *Of Human Bondage,* Lenny in Steinbeck's *Of Mice and Men,* and Caroline Dummer in Cozzens' *By Love Possessed,* to name a few. The hill people of *Deliverance,* Mr. Singer in McCuller's *The Heart is a Lonely Hunter,* and Charly in Daniel Keyes' *Flowers for Algernon,* are but a small sampling of films in which disabled characters have played major and minor roles.

Some media treat disabilities sensitively and fairly. Most do not. Our central questions are: in what ways have literature and electronic media created or intensified societal prejudices, stereotypes, and ultimately, discrimination; in what ways have they dealt with disabilities humanistically? We ask these questions not to create formulas for fair and sensitive portrayals. Art needs no formulas. Rather, we

2

ask them in order to heighten our awareness of handicapism in culture and to provide insights into how cultural media can contribute to greater understanding and acceptance of disabilities. What follows is a typology of disability-related stereotypes in media:

THE SINISTER DISABLED: Captain Hook and Long John Silver are examples of famous characters who are made to appear all the more evil because of their physical disabilities. Captain Ahab in *Moby Dick* fits the same mold. The villain "Injun" Joe in Mark Twain's *Tom Sawyer* has a limp. The sinister stereotype also emerges in filmdom's demonic and fascistic Dr. Strangelove in Stanley Kubrick's *Dr. Strangelove,* and in less caricatured forms in the hangman of Mel Brooks' *Blazing Saddles,* the midget Dr. Lovelace in *Wild, Wild West* and, upon occasion, as villains in Sherlock Holmes thrillers. It is almost as if script writers had read the early works of the physical anthropologist Lombroso, who claimed a clear relationship between certain physiological characteristics (broad foreheads, fallen chins, thick lips and the like) and criminality. Horror movies usually associate hunchbacks and other physically different-looking people with evil, but even more particularly, with degenerate behavior. The image of monster men attacking defenseless women recurs frequently in such films. A particularly offensive aspect of this stereotype is that villains are frequently portrayed as less intelligent than their pursuers; the implication is that criminal behavior derives from "low intelligence."

Classic literature has also featured disabled villains. Illustrations for the Grimm Brothers' "Rumpelstiltskin" often depict the evil Rumpelstiltskin as a very small man with a hump on his back, balding head, large nose and pointed ears. In addition, the deformed witch in Hansel and Gretel must also be disabled — she used crutches to perpetrate her wickedness.

VICTIMS OF VIOLENCE: People with disabilities have also been portrayed in roles directly contradictory to that of the sinister, depraved and criminal type. So it is that people with disabilities are cast as defenseless recipients of violence. "The Ugly Duckling" presents this role model in its classic form, that of the different being taken as fair prey by those who consider themselves normal. In the context of discrimination and prejudice, "normal" is superior. "The Ugly Duckling," however, like so many fairy tales, fortunately provides in a final scene a stroke of poetic justice.

"The Little Humpbacked Horse" is a Russian fairytale which also features a reversal (Wheeler). In this tale, Ivan the Dullard is endowed with unusual honesty and a little humpbacked horse that has magical powers. In part, we are treated to the usual theme of special gifts or powers being hidden in the least suspected places, in this case in the disabled dullard and in the humpbacked horse. But throughout the story, another stereotypic role returns again and again: that of the different or disabled person as victim of violence. Repeatedly, the Tzar requires Ivan the Dullard to enter extremely difficult challenges, and each time to face certain death as the penalty for failure:

If in three days thou hast not brought hither, from the hidden valley of the Land of the South, the Pig with the Golden Bristles and Silver Tusks, together with her twenty sucklings, I will deliver thee to an evil death!

Heed my royal word. If in seven days thou has not brought hither from between the crystal hills of the Caucasus the Seven-Maned Mare with her seven stallions, I will send thee where the crows shall pick thy bones!

bring...the lovely Girl-Tzar within twelve days or pay the forfeit with ...(your) head.

Finally, the Tzar bids Ivan the Dullard to bathe in three cauldrons, one of cold water, one of boiling water and the third of boiling milk. The humpbacked horse saved Ivan from death by scalding, but provides no such magic for the Tzar, who expires in the boiling liquids. Simple honesty prevails over greed.

Other examples of the same stereotype are numerous. The mildly retarded hill people in *Deliverance* are at once the perpetrators and victims of a violent struggle with a few weekend campers. Steinbeck's Lenny in *Of Mice and Men* murders and is murdered. The blind heroine of *Wait Until Dark* (Knott), finally outwits a series of thugs who invade her apartment in search of a valuable cache, but only after they have thoroughly terrorized her. In the fashion of several of the fairy tales mentioned above, there is poetic justice here too. The deaf Mr. Singer in Carson Mc-Culler's *The Heart Is a Lonely Hunter* becomes a confidant with whom several main characters share their personal struggles. But finally he succumbs to suicide when he can find no satisfactory outlet for his own feelings. And Singer's friend Antanapoulos, who is deaf, unable to speak, and retarded, dies in an institution.

Calling such portrayals stereotypical oversimplifies them. The problem with literary and cinematic portrayal of people with disabilities as victims of violence is not one of exaggeration or dishonesty; people with disabilities do suffer victimization. The problem lies in the kinds of victimization portrayed. Overwhelmingly, the arts have portrayed violence between individuals rather than violence at the hands of social institutions (e.g., unemployment, institutionalization, or poverty). Yet this latter form is the more frequent experience of those who are disabled. The one area in which writers and filmmakers have broken this paradigm of individual violence to examine the violence within social institutions is that of mental illness. Marge Piercy's *Woman on the Edge of Time* and Ken Kesey's *One Flew Over the Cuckoo's Nest* explore the abuses of mental hospitals and contemporary forms of mind control.

THE EXTRAORDINARY DISABLED: At the opposite end of the spectrum we find another set of stereotypes. These are the romantic, the idealized, and the overstated. It is perhaps predictable that in the same culture which portrays people with disabilities as burdensome, we should find images at the other extremes —

the super disabled. Just as racist stereotypes include the pathetic, lazy, dumb, black person, so too do they include the sexually virile, intelligent, and physically superior "superfly." The extraordinary disabled are found largely in television. This electronic medium has spawned a number of disabled heroes, each possessing an extraordinary skill to compensate for a disability. It sometimes seems that the disabled person has even been assigned a magical quality. Television's super detectives "Longstreet," who cannot see, developed such a keen sense of hearing that he becomes indeed all-seeing. Though paralyzed, "Ironsides" had extraordinary reasoning power which sometimes amounted to a sixth sense. More recently "bionic" superheroes have taken center stage as the extraordinary disabled.

In literature, Charly in Keyes' *Flowers for Algernon* achieves extraordinary capability temporarily, though only when he sheds his retardation through medical intervention.

ETERNAL CHILDREN: Too often movies about people who are retarded — there has been a spate of such movies in the last few years — portray their disabled main characters as "gee-golly," happy-go-lucky simpletons. Even the titles of some of these films — the use of first names like "Charly" and "Larry" — evoke this image. The original Daniel Keyes novel, *Flowers for Algernon,* upon which the movie "Charly" was based, portrays the retarded person an an ingenuous, clownish character. To the author's credit, the main character is also shown as someone who has been mistreated and wrongly conditioned (especially by professionals) — an accurate reflection of society's molding of retarded people into these roles. The important point is that stories must begin to communicate to readers that retarded adults are not necessarily foot-shuffling, "gee-golly," happy-go-lucky people. Retarded adults experience the same emotions as non-disabled people, are capable of a broad range of behaviors, and possess individual and complex personalities. The recent film *Best Boy* portrays this more humanistic view of people with retardation. Much of the "Disabled adult as child" image comes from the concept of "mental age." Retarded adults are sometimes assigned mental ages of children. And this leads to the colloquiallism, "He looks like an adult, but he has the mind of an 8-year-old." It should be noted that the concept of mental age is a grossly inadequate and misleading way of describing mental retardation. "Larry," a 1974 television film, accepts the eternal child image. It is based on the true story of a person who as a baby was placed in an institution for retarded people. Years later, after having grown up in the institution and having learned institutional behavior (shuffling his feet, slurring his words so that they seem unintelligible), he was "discovered." Officials at the institution at last realized that he had normal intelligence. In a moving, though typically melodramatic manner, the film portrays Larry's transformation from an institutionalized person to a socialized person. A review for *The New York Times* called the character Larry a man-child. Interestingly, we are told that Larry can become a man and can move out into the community because he is *not* retarded. Presumably, were he not diagnosed as normal, he would have been left in the institution. Indeed, all the other residents of the institution are portrayed as childlike. The institution's staff play children's games with the resident grown men, as if the men were perpetual children, unable to benefit either from education or from being treated as adults. "Larry" denies overwhelmingly evidence that all people, no matter how severe their impairments, can learn. The film presents the moving story of one man's escape from retardation and an institutional nexus, while it quietly and with terribly powerful understatement confirms the mythical "eternal child" imagery which haunts people labeled "retarded."

OUTSIDERS AND INTERESTING SCENERY: In some television programs disabled characters are "thrown in" much as one might incorporate unusual objects in the scenery, such as Columbo's old car or his rumpled raincoat. An example is Chester in the classic "Gunsmoke" series, who has an otherwise marginal role in the show. Many stories and television programs include a blind musician or a blind newspaper man. The roles of midgets in television and film frequently provide extra interest but have no additional purpose.

We can hypothesize that midgets and blind musicians or newsdealers are cast into film and television to provide an exotic element. Perhaps, these are simply more modest forms of P.T. Barnum's early sideshows. In any case, whether or not we can establish that a new sideshow has emerged, the practice of using disabled people to "spice up" a film set denies the humanity of people with disabilities by reducing them to curious objects.

INCOMPETENT BURDENS: A common stereotype imposed by society is that of the disabled person as sick, incompetent, or severely less competent than a "normal" dependent person.

There are two extremes to the incompetent burden stereotype — at one end the laughable Mr. Magoo and at the other, the tragic figure of Lenny in Steinbeck's *Of Mice and Men.* Mr. Magoo is the quintessential fool the ultimate caricature of society's belief that disabled people are, in some tragic-comic way, humorous and laughable. Magoo bumps and stumbles through life, scrunching up against doors, lamp posts and myriad other objects which stand waiting to spell his doom.

To press the comic element, Magoo survives it all, somehow, unaware that he walks through a veritable minefield of potential disasters each moment he is on the screen. Although he survives, his survival is a result of good luck and fate, not competence. Indeed, we are led to believe that his incompetence gives him special license to survive unscathed a variety of situations that would decimate any able-bodied person.

The Magoo character is neither new nor alone. Jerry Lewis' early contortion, somewhat akin to the notion of a person who has cerebral palsy, solicited wide laughter from the Dean Martin/Jerry Lewis audiences. Television comedians who stutter evoke the same response.

At the other end of the extreme burdensome helplessness enters. Sarason discusses this role extensively in a chapter of this book when he examines Bellow's *Something Happened.* Consequently we will examine another treatment of the burdensome role.

Dalton Trumbo's *Johnny Got His Gun,* a classic anti-war novel written in

1939, presents the issue of burdensomeness in quite another light. Trumbo rejects the stereotype. He treats the stereotype not as a fair reflection of a disabled person, but as society's inhuman imposition upon people who have disabilities. In an heroic way, he calls for normalizing the relationships of disabled and nondisabled people. War took all but the ultimate toll on Trumbo's main character, Johnny. He lost most of his face, including his eyes, nose, mouth, ears, chin, and his legs and arms in battle. Yet he remains a thinking, feeling, caring person. The book combines reminiscences of his experiences prior to the war, and of his life as a nameless former soldier in a nameless hospital. After five years of lying in bed, he has learned how to communicate. His discovery of a way to communicate by tapping out code messages with his head against his pillow, is finally recognized by his captors. He taps them a message: he wants out of the hospital. He promises to cause no trouble; that he can raise money by providing a kind of sideshow to support himself. He wants to be out among people; he wants to tell them about war. He wants to be free. He wants to live productively, to contribute to the people and the world around him. But when a man in the hospital finally taps back a message, it is a product of bureaucracy, not of compassion:

W H A T

Y O U

A S K

I S

A G A I N S T

R E G U L A T I O N S

W H O

A R E

Y O U

He could almost hear the wail of pain that went up from his heart. It was a sharp terrible personal pain, the kind of pain that comes only when someone to whom you have never done any harm turns on you and says goodbye forever without any reason for doing it. Without any reason at all.

He had done nothing to them. He wasn't to blame for the trouble he was causing yet they were drawing the curtain around him stuffing him back into the womb back into the grave saying to him goodbye don't bother us don't come back to life the dead should stay dead and we are done with you.

But why?

He had hurt no one. He had tried to give them as little trouble as possible. He was a great care that was true but he hadn't intentionally become so. He wasn't a thief or a drunkard or a liar or a murderer. He was a man no worse no better than anybody else. He was just a guy who'd had to go to war who'd been hurt bad and now was trying to get out from his prison to feel fresh cool air on his skin to sense the color and movement of people around him. That was all he wanted. And to him who had harmed nobody they were saying goodnight goodbye stay where you are don't give us any trouble you are beyond life you are beyond death you are even beyond hope you are gone you are finished forever goodnight and goodbye.

Why should he be a prisoner? he had committed no crime. What right had they to keep him? What possible reason could they have to be so inhuman to him?

Why? Why? Why?

Conclusion

"Ugly" is a label. It arbitrarily and subjectively defines a physical condition. And, even when "accurate" — that is, when there is wide agreement that the label has been appropriately applied — it is rarely helpful to the person so stamped. Most labels do more harm than good. Disability labels such as "mentally retarded," "blind," "deaf," "physically disabled," "emotionally disturbed" and "learning disabled," like the labels "ugly," "fat," or "short," presumably have their origins primarily as descriptive terms, and are applied to people who appear or behave in ways that are considered to be different from some social norms. Yet, as we have begun to explore, such labels carry with them a variety of additonal cultural messages. In the context of cultural media, disability labels often act as cues for images of dependence and helplessness, pathos, pity, guilt, love and sorrow, tragedy, incompetence, unusual personality formations, sexlessness, sexual deviance and excessive sexuality, magical powers, criminality, and saintliness. Whether positive or negative, stereotypes prove debilitating to disabled persons. The individual's humanity is obscured in the anonymity of unidimensional characterizations.

WORKS CITED

Anderson, Hans C. *The Ugly Duckling.*New York: Scroll Press, 1975.

Biklen, Douglas, and Robert Bogdan. "Handicapism." *Social Policy,* March/April, 1977, 14-19.

Brooks, Mel, dir. *Blazing Saddles.* With Cleaven Little and Gene Wilder. Warner Bros., 1974.

Barrie, J.M. *Peter Pan.* New York: Scribner's, 1904.

Cozzens, James G. *By Love Possessed.* New York: Fawcett, 1977.

Dickens, Charles. *A Christmas Carol.* 1843; rpt. New York: Dutton, 1972.

Dickey, James, *Deliverance.* New York: Dell, 1971.

Dostoyevsky, Feodor. *The Idiot.* 1868; rpt. New York: Dell, 1962.

The Grimm Brothers. *The Complete Grimm's Fairytales.* New York: Pantheon, 1974.

Hugo, Victor. *The Hunchback of Notre Dame.* 1831; rpt. New York: Dutton, 1953.

Kesey, Ken. *One Flew Over the Cuckoo's Nest.* New York: Penguin, 1976.

Keyes, Daniel. *Flowers for Algernon.* New York: Bantam, 1970.

Knott, Frederick, *Wait Until Dark.* Film directed by Terence Young, with Audrey Hepburn, Warner Bros., 1967.

Kubrick, Stanley, dir. *Dr. Strangelove: How I Learned to Stop Worrying and Love the Bomb.* With Peter Sellers, Columbia Pictures, 1964.

"Larry" (New York: Learning Corporation of America, 1974), 16 mm film.

Lorenzini, Carlo ("Collodi") *Pinocchio.* 1883.

Maugham, Somerset. *Of Human Bondage.* 1915; rpt. New York: Penguin, 1978.

McCuller, Carson. *The Heart Is a Lonely Hunter.* New York: Bantam, 1970.

Melville, Herman. *Moby Dick*. 1851; rpt. New York: Abrams, 1976.

Piercy, Marge. *Woman on the Edge of Time*. New York: Fawcett, 1978.

Shakespeare, William. "King Richard III." *The Complete Works of Shakespeare*. London: Oxford University Press, 1943.

Spyri, Johanna. *Heidi*. New York: MacMillan, 1962.

Steinbeck, John. *Of Mice and Men*. 1937; rpt. New York: Bantam, 1970.

Trumbo, Dalton. *Johnny Got His Gun*. New York: Bantam, 1970.

Twain, Mark. *Tom Sawyer*. 1876; rpt. Bridgeport, CT: Airmont, 1979.

Wheeler, Post. "The Little Humpbacked Horse." *Russian Wonder Tales*. New York: Yoseloff, 1957.

IMAGES OF DISABILITY IN ART
by Sidney Thomas

I don't need to argue, I think, the importance or the power of visual images in determining our attitudes on any subject, whether on handicappism or racism, sexism or any other key problem that we deal with today. However, I think it is necessary at the beginning to make several disclaimers. Visual images in themselves do not determine our attitudes toward the handicapped and toward disability. These attitudes are determined basically by social factors, by the nature of the society in which we live, by what we do about the problems of the handicapped. What visual images do is, first, to reinforce these attitudes, to give them a power, a vividness, which they may not otherwise have; second, to define for us perhaps more effectively, perhaps more powerfully than anything else, exactly what the attitudes of society are.

In looking at the visual images of disability for any time, any place, any society, we discover what that society thinks about disability, what that society does about disability, and it's in that context that I want to deal with some of the more famous of the images of disability that we have had in European art over the centuries. These images are of many different kinds. Many of them are stereotypes; many of them represent not an honest, truthful attempt to deal with disability in human terms, but rather stereotypes that are part of the unconscious or partly conscious thinking of the particular society. Other images, of course, represent a more original, a more honest attempt to come to grips with the particular problems of disability the artist is concerned with.

I'd like to begin with one of the most famous of all images of disability in European art, and also one of the best examples of what we mean by a stereotype. It is an image that does not come to grips with the material it pretends to deal with, but rather an image that simply reinforces certain pat assumptions. Figure One* is a painting by the 19th century English painter, John E. Millais, one of a group of painters known as the Pre-Raphaelites, active in the 1850's and 1860's. It is known as "The Blind Girl". What we see is an image of blindness which deals not with the situation of the human being afflicted with the disability of blindness or attempting to cope with it, nor in any real sense with our own attitudes toward blindness, but one which simply sentimentalizes the problem and creates a fake pathos. Every part of the image tends to create this false pathos, attempts to make us feel that we are sympathetically engaged with the problem, when in reality we are very far away from it. The rainbow, for example, the symbol of hope in the distance, the placement of the blind girl in a colorful, attractive landscape, the vivid,

*See Appendix A.

deliberately "beautiful" colors of the painting—all of these make for a false glamor and tend to rob the whole situation of the blind girl of the power, the humanity, the significance which it truly has, reducing it to a sentimental image which we can in a sense enjoy because we feel that we're involved with the problem when in reality we are making no real contact with it.

I want to turn now to an image of a completely different kind. In Doug Biklen's slide presentation on "Handicapism" we had at the beginning of this symposium, one of the problems dealt with was that of ugliness, and society's attitude toward ugliness: the way in which, particularly in our modern society, we look at physical ugliness as a kind of symbol of moral corruption, in which we make the ugly individual a monster, in which we cease to look at him as a human being, in which we glorify physical beauty as a value in itself. Figure Two is a painting of the Italian Renaissance done in the 1480's by a painter called Domenico Ghirlandaio, who incidentally was the teacher of Michelangelo. The painting represents an old man and a young child, presumably his grandchild. What is interesting to me is that this painting, done in an age which in many ways glorified physical beauty even more than ours does, at the same time was able to accept ugliness and deformity, to accept it in a human being without robbing the human being of his humanity. You see, of course, the terribly deformed nose, that strawberry nose, the warts on the face, as also the agedness of the old man, age again being in our modern society a handicap, and yet, what the painting communicates is the sense of the human relationship between the old and the young, the grandfather and the grandson, in a very moving way, and in a way which, to my mind, escapes the sentimentality and the falsity of the Millais image.

"The Club Footed Boy" (Fig. 3) is perhaps the most famous image of disability in the history of European art. When I told a colleague of mine yesterday that I was going to speak today on images of disability in European art, her immediate reaction was to say, "What else is there besides Ribera's "Club-Footed Boy?" This is the one image of disability which every art historian is able immediately to think of. Incidentally, the fact that she could think only of this one image, that her concept of disability did not extend beyond this, is in itself, I believe, a mark of handicappism, a sign of inability to recognize the extraordinary range of handicaps, and disabilities that are part of modern society. Jusepe Ribera, was a Spanish painter of the 17th century, who spent most of his career in Naples, and the painting is known as the "Club-footed Boy." It represents a young boy confronting us directly, and holding in his left hand a paper which says, "Give me charity for the love of God." And what we have in this image, I think, are two approaches to disability, one a positive approach, one a negative approach. The negative approach, of course, is the injunction to charity, the implication that the only recourse of this handicapped boy is an appeal to charity. But the positive aspect of this is that Ribera, a great painter, a man with extraordinary feeling for human beings as human beings, is able to create in the pose and expression of this boy a sense of courage, of assurance, of individuality. The boy is not simply an object of chari-

12

ty, but an individual who asserts himself, an individual with *life,* a feeling that he belongs in his own world despite his deformity, a feeling almost of a kind of deliberate self-assurance and jaunty confidence.

Ribera is also the artist of another remarkable painting of disability, a painting which I had the good fortune to see recently in London in a special exhibit of Spanish painting, a painting which not only I, but very few other people, have ever had the opportunity to see before, since it's in a remote collection in a provincial town of Spain. It is a painting of a bearded woman, the kind of individual who is usually an object of fun, a freak in a circus, who, because of her particular kind of disability, is looked upon as no longer a human being. The remarkable thing about that painting by Ribera, and what made it the real success of that entire exhibit, was the dignity with which Ribera was able to present the bearded woman, the fact that he showed her to us no longer as a freak, but again as a human being with her own individuality, her own self respect and right to exist.

Let's turn now to one of the most remarkable and powerful images of disability ever created by any painter. This is a work by the great 17th century Spanish painter, Diego Velazquez, one of the greatest painters in the history of western art. It is a painting of a dwarf, a man named Sebastian de Morra (Fig. 4). The Spanish court in the 17th century collected dwarves and deformed individuals as a kind of circus for themselves, as a way of entertaining themselves by surrounding themselves with individuals upon whom they could look as objects of fun, whom they could enjoy almost as their own personal dolls, their own puppets. One of these dwarves was this individual, Sebastian De Morra, painted by Velazquez, who was the royal painter. Notice what Velazquez has done. He has deliberately painted Sebastian seated in order to conceal as much as possible the deformity from which he suffers, in order to give him as much dignity and individuality as possible. Velazquez as a great painter is projecting to us the emotions of Sebastian de Morra, his feeling not simply of his own situation as a human being, but the fierceness with which he looks out at this world that had degraded him, that has transformed him, in a sense, into a nonperson. To me, this is one of the most powerful, one of the most moving of all the paintings of the 17th century. I was looking just the other day at a standard work on Velazquez, done by the leading living authority on his art. In discussing this particular painting, the author of the book refers to the way Velazquez has caught the "petulant" expression of Sebastian de Morra. Now, to apply the term "petulant" to Sebastian is to treat him as a child, as an infant who is having a kind of tantrum while he's being painted; it is to treat him not for what he is, but what the author of the book thinks he is, which is I think about as good an example of what was called handicappism earlier in this symposium as anything I can think of.

Let's look now to the painter who more than any other painter in the history of art conveys an attitude of understanding and support, of shared humanity toward the handicapped, whether the handicap is old age, blindness, or any other. This is Rembrandt, the great Dutch painter of the 17th century, and of course the fact that Rembrandt, more than any other painter in the history of art, creates positive images of disability is a reflection not simply of Rembrandt's quality, but of the society which he represents, the Dutch bourgeois society of the 17th century. It's no accident that the same country, the same era that produced Rembrandt, produced also the first society in the history of Europe that practiced as well as preached true religious toleration, and opened its quarters to the Jews who had been expelled from other countries of Europe, treating them as full citizens; in many ways, it was superior in its practice of human rights to any society that had existed in Europe up to that time.

Figure Five is a painting of Rembrandt's mother, done when Rembrandt was still a relatively young man. Rembrandt was obsessed, one might say, with images of old age from his youth on. During his entire painting career of more than forty years, again and again he returns to the subject of old age, because to Rembrandt, throughout all of his career, old age signified what unfortunately it no longer signifies in our society. It signified wisdom, the profound summation of a lifetime of experience; it signified something not simply to be tolerated, but something to be respected and admired; it signified not a disability, but rather a positive achievement. And here in one of Rembrandt's first images of old age, I think we can see this clearly.

What Rembrandt gives us above all in his treatments of old age is his own image (Fig. 6). As he grew older he painted himself again and again, and in particular in the last twelve years or so of his life, he painted his greatest self-portraits, himself as an old man, but an old man neither to be pitied nor sentimentalized nor idealized. He paints himself with all of the disabilities of old age—the pouches under the eyes, the sagging jowls, the wrinkles, the sense of physical weariness; but at the same time he presents himself to us as someone who has come to terms with his old age, someone in whom the positive qualities of old age, experience, wisdom and so on, are projected with a profundity, an inner contemplation that no other painter has ever achieved. Here, for example, in the so-called Ilchester self-portrait, he has deliberately, with tongue in cheek, presented himself to us as a kind of monarch, seated in a throne-like chair with his mahl stick, one of the tools of the painter, held like a scepter, with the cap on his head like the crown of a king, and with a sense, as he looks at us, that he is equal in quality to any individual of his own society.

Now here is another image of old age, again painted by Rembrandt, in the last decade of his life in 1661 (Fig. 7). This is an old man praying, and once again, Rembrandt does not in any way avoid the physical deterioration of old age. Here again there is no sentimentalizing of the image, but once more the inner contemplation, the profundity of vision, the wisdom, the experience of old age is what concerns Rembrandt. Figure Eight is "Jacob Blessing the Sons of Joseph," and again we have the patriarchal image, a painting of the unified family in which every individual within the family has his or her realm. The grandfather, the son, the daughter-in-law, the grandchildren, all are part of the same family group, each one with his or her own place and function within the family. This is a painting that could only have developed in a society in which respect for all members of the family, the aged as well as the young, was an integral part of the society. Certainly what we have here is one of the most beautiful treatments of that whole complex of family relationships, and above all, the dignity, the worth of the aged member, the grandfather Jacob.

Here is perhaps the greatest of Rembrandt's paintings, "The Return of the Prodigal Son" (Fig. 9). The parable of the Prodigal Son particularly attracted Rembrandt because it contained within itself the sense of the importance of human relationships, which was always significant for Rembrandt. It is, of course, the story of the son who leaves his father and his home to live a life of dissipation, who ruins himself, spends his inheritance and returns physically destroyed, in absolute poverty, to his father, and whom his father welcomes back, celebrating by killing the fatted calf. The other son, the good son who has always lived properly and done his duty, bitterly objects to the killing of the fatted calf for this son who has wasted his life in dissipation, and the father answers, "He who is lost is found again." Here you see the son embraced by the father, and again one sees age not as decrepitude to be taken care of, to be endured as a burden, but rather, as a source of comfort for the young, the aged suckling the young, the embrace of the father enfolding the son in all of his poverty, in all of his despair, as he is brought back into the family relationship.

Finally, in the work of Rembrandt, Figure Ten is the painting that Rembrandt was working on at the time of his death. It was found on his easel when he died; it is Simeon holding the Christ child in the temple. Rembrandt was a deeply religious man and his culture was a deeply religious culture; but it was a culture which emphasized the humanization of religion and of religious ideas. Here the blind old Simeon holding the infant Jesus is represented not as someone deprived because of his blindness and age, but gifted with an inner vision that enables him to recognize and receive the divine infant.

I want now to turn to another kind of image of blindness, a work by the Flemish painter, Pieter Bruegel the Elder, "The Blind Leading the Blind" (Fig. 11). Here is a quite different vision of blindness from Rembrandt's. It's not blindness as contributing to a kind of inner vision, but blindness as a symbol of human folly, as a symbol of the traps which human beings set for themselves. At first sight it is a frightening, almost brutal treatment of blindness as we look at the deformed, distorted figures and faces of these blind individuals, each one leading the other into further disaster. But there's also an honesty about this vision of blindness, also a reality about it, for it tells us what Bruegel's society thought of the blind. While it is not an image that attracts us, but an image that repels us, it's also an image that shows us what society can do to disabled individuals. And it forms, of course, a striking contrast with the Rembrandt image that we have just seen.

An even more terrible image is Figure Twelve, by the Spanish painter, Goya, of the late 18th and early 19th century. This is one of the paintings Goya did in his old age on the walls of his villa outside of Madrid, the so-called "House of the Deaf Man". It is a painting of two old people eating, and just as in the Bruegel painting where we found a contrast to the Rembrandt conception of the blind individual, here we see a contrast with the Rembrandt conception of old age. Old age is no longer something honored but is something terrifying. These two aged individuals, reduced simply to greed, live for nothing else but the satisfaction of their greed, and create a terrifying vision of humanity, one which reduces human beings to an animal level. Once again we have a painting which is important to confront, because it represents a significant aspect of society's attitude toward disabled people. It represents an attitude we have to deal with if we're going to be able to change the situation of the handicapped. Of course, what this painting represents is not so much old age as such, but old age as a symbol for Goya of what has happened to humanity generally in his own time. It's only one of a number of horrifying images that Goya painted on the wall of his House of the Deaf Man, images in which younger people are just as terrifying, just as frightening, so here the disability becomes a symbol of a larger disillusionment on the part of Goya with his own society.

Figure Thirteen is a painting of a different kind by the great French romantic painter, Theodore Gericault, done about 1822-1823. It is a painting of a mad-woman, and what it represents is the first attempt in the history of western art to deal with mental illness not as something either to be laughed at or as something to recoil from in horror, but as a human situation to be confronted as we would deal with any human problem. Gericault was commissioned by a friend named Dr. Georget, a psychiatrist, to do a series of portraits of insane people. According to Georget's theory, every type of insanity, every type of mental illness was characterized by a particular facial expression. A person suffering from one type of delusion would look different from someone with another type of mental illness. Important to us today is not this outdated kind of psychiatry, but the way in which Gericault as a true artist was able to go beyond Georget's theories to give us for the first time a truly human portrait of an individual suffering from mental disability.

Up to this time, of course, in art as well as in society, mentally ill people were treated, as I said before, either as objects of fun or horror. Goya, in the 1790's, painted a picture of a madhouse which communicates that kind of quality. Many of you are familiar with the play known in its short title as "Marat-Sade" which is set in an asylum for the mentally ill in France at the time of the French Revolution, and are therefore familiar with the way in which mentally ill people are represented in that play as they were treated in the 18th century. To me, this is one of the most significant portraits of the 19th century, not simply for its own quality, but for what it represents in terms of a step forward for human beings in the treatment of other human beings.

Now I want to jump almost a full century to the greatest image-maker of the 20th century, the Spanish painter Pablo Picasso. Most people think of Picasso in terms primarily of his cubist paintings, his semi-abstract paintings, his more experimental paintings of his later years. But let us look at Picasso, who, as a young man, arrived in Paris without money, without resources and lived for a number of years a life of almost complete destitution. His early paintings, the paintings of his so-called blue period, from about 1900 to about 1904, deal again and again with poor people, handicapped people, and disabled people. For example, the painting known simply as "The Blind Man" (Fig. 14) does not communicate to us a shallow sympathy for the blind man. It is the sense of his existence and worth as a human being that makes this one of Picasso's finest early paintings.

Figure Fifteen is another painting dealing with an image of disability: "The Old Guitarist,'" sometimes known as "The Blind Guitarist." It combines in its imagery two kinds of disability, age and blindness. Once again, Picasso has conveyed great power, great understanding, great humanity.

In this painting of a dwarf (Fig. 16) I have no doubt that Picasso was thinking of many of Velazquez's paintings of dwarves done three centuries earlier, and again, what I like about this work is the defiance. This is not someone who is asking for our pity, but a person looking out at us with a kind of anger, a feeling for her own status as a human being. It's this quality which links it with the Velazquez painting of Sebastian De Morra that we examined earlier (Fig. 4).

Now, Figure Seventeen is a painting of Picasso's last years. This is one of a number of paintings which Picasso did about 1963 or 1964, dealing with the theme of the artist and his model, in which, of course, he himself is the artist, and his model is his wife of that particular period. What I enjoy about all of these paintings on this theme is the fact that Picasso, when he painted this particular work at the age of 82 or 83, is not yielding to any kind of self-pity for himself, but is projecting in his own image and in the way he is responding to the new image beside him, his sense of the joy of life, the joy of creativity. This sense is something which he managed to retain to the very end of his life, even in paintings he was doing as late as the early 1970's, shortly before his death over age 90.

It's this quality which we see also in a Picasso painting of the same period known as "The Family" (Fig. 18). There he is in the center surrounded by various figures not necessarily of his own family, but of what constitutes a complete family. Notice the range of ages, from the old man seated in the center to the woman at his left, and then the younger woman at the other side: the sense of the family ranging from the youngest to the oldest as a symbol of the completeness of human life.

I return now to Rembrandt and to one of his latest paintings known simply as "The Family Group" (Fig. 19), which again gives us a complete image of the human family. Notice that there is no image of disability in it; there is no handicapped individual in this painting. It may seem strange to you that I end with this painting and with one of the last paintings done by Goya, a work known as "The Milkmaid of Bordeaux" (Fig. 20). Why should I conclude with these two paintings in a discussion of images of disability in art? The reason is this: the question I think is bound to be asked as we deal with the way in which artists have dealt with images of disability is: how can they deal with them in such a way as to fight handicappism, to create a positive attitude toward human beings no matter what their handicap?

I think the answer is, that *to the extent artists deliberately set out to paint positive images of disabled people, to that extent they fail really to fight handicappism.* What they create is almost bound to be a kind of shallow propaganda painting, one that is not really felt either by the artist or by the spectator. The way for the artist to fight handicappism is to do what the artist can do better than any one else—that is, to express a sense of the creative possibilities of human life, to express a sense of the dignity of human beings, their individuality, their worth, whether handicapped or not, whether old or young. In the painting Goya did just a few months before his death in his 80's, of a beautiful young girl he had come to know in his exile in Bordeaux, what strikes us is the joy of creativity, the feeling that Goya has restored in himself his faith in humanity which in the paintings in the House of the Deaf Man he seems to have lost forever. It's through this feeling for human beings, this explosion of creative ardor and joy upon the part of the artist that I think he or she can do most to fight against any semblance of handicappism, either within the artist or in the society that the artist addresses.

18

TEARS, LAUGHS, AND THE BEST FOOT FORWARD
by John D. Diehl

There must be at least as many ways of dealing with physical handicaps in literature as there are authors who are involved with them. Various indeed are the ways, and dependent on a host of things: the nature of the society which produced the author; the author's own personality and values; the personality and values of characters written about; the spirit of the literary work; the nature and severity of the handicap; and the origin of the handicap—is it congenital or acquired, and if acquired, how acquired, and how recently?

Take, for instance, reactions to the lack of a leg. The irascible Peter Stuyvesant who figures so prominently in Washington Irving's largely fanciful *Knickerbocker's History of New York* has, in Irving's words,

> an accidental advantage, with which I am surprised that neither Homer nor Virgil have graced any of their houses. This was nothing less than a wooden leg, which was the only prize he had gained in bravely fighting the battles of his country, but of which he was so proud, that he was often heard to declare he valued it more than all his other limbs put together; indeed so highly did he esteem it, that he had it gallantly enchased and relieved with silver devices, which caused it to be related in diverse histories and legends that he wore a silver leg.

Quite different is the reaction of monomaniacal Captain Ahab of Herman Melville's *Moby Dick,* who wears an ivory leg:

> Aye aye! it was that accursed white whale that razed me; made a poor begging lumber of me forever and a day! . . . Aye, aye! and I'll chase him round Good Hope, and round the Horn, and round the Norway Malestrom, and round perdition's flames before I give him up . . . He tasks me; he heaps me; I see in him outrageous strength, with an inscrutable malice sinewing it. That inscrutable thing is chiefly what I hate; and be the white whale agent, or be the white whale principal, I will wreak that hate upon him.

Unlike either Peter Stuyvesant or Captain Ahab is Robert Louis Stevenson's Long John Silver, who seems to have been the same engaging, resourceful rogue before he lost his leg that he is when embarked on the journey to Treasure Island. He, like the two other men I have mentioned, does seem extraordinarily active—as a compensation, we might think, for partial disablement. But there is no suggestion of hyperactivity as the result of being maimed in Thomas Hood's short poem about Ben Battles:

Ben Battles was a soldier bold,
     And used to war's alarms.
A cannonball took off his legs,
     So he lay down his arms.

Obviously these illustrations do not exhaust the ways in which the loss of legs or a leg can be responded to. Undoubtedly disorientation and despair figure in the typical immediate reactions of those actually faced with such a traumatic loss. But no one responce can exhaust the possible responses, or, further, be assumed to be that of a person born without a limb or the use of it.

Most writers in whose works images of physical handicap occur have not themselves been physically handicapped, above and beyond suffering from possible slight negative variations from the norm in eyesight, hearing, strength, stamina, speed, or something else. Most writers are not physically handicapped to the degree of difference which gives meaning to the term "handicapped." Because they aren't handicapped, most writers tend to approach dealing with handicaps from the outside. They observe handicaps in others, or project their own fears and fantasies into characters they may invent. This is natural enough; for we all, non-handicapped and handicapped alike, start out from ourselves and our own experience. But there is just so much we can learn by observation and fantasies. And it can bother the writer. Just how can he create, say, a convincing lame man? How does a lame man actually feel? A kindred problem is felt in life by all who are comparatively able-bodied and don't know how to behave with the unknown in the form of a lame man. Should we hold his arm? Should we open the door for him? Should we let him flounder on self-reliantly by himself? Should we try to kick him out of the way? Our own experience again will teach us something. And so will literature. We can probably learn most authentically by listening to what lame men themselves have to say, in life and in letters.

Most physically handicapped writers have not written on the subject of being physically handicapped, or written exclusively or primarily on the subject. They have had other fish to fry. Physical handicap is not the only subject of interest to a handicapped person, or even the principal subject of interest. Like everyone else, the handicapped person can be beset with family problems, religious doubts, vocational uncertainties, and financial worries. Able-bodied people often fail to realize this and thus may be implicitly denying the full humanity of the physically handicapped. The latter, too, enjoy (if that's the word for it) the same right as the able-bodied to be baffled, confused, antagonized, indifferent, enthusiastic, and disillusioned about matters other than handicaps. Handicaps are part, but not all of the world of the handicapped.

I would guess that those of us alive now in the western world are in a better position to understand what life means and can mean to the handicapped than previous generations of humankind were. It is part of the growing inward orientation of the western world that we are more able now and often more willing to listen to the subjective complaints and aspirations of a kind of person who in earlier centuries could not, did not speak out so boldly and explicitly about matters so extremely close to him. And it is part of the continuing, in some ways growing, external orientation of the west that we can see very individual problems and achievements as matters of general importance.

It's all to the good that we can do so. A physical handicap is a drawback; it would be a drawback for the handicapped person even if he lived on a desert island. Robinson Crusoe surely would not have been as well off on his Island of Despair if his eyesight had been markedly less keen, his ambulatory powers severely limited. But the effects of being handicapped can be even worse in society than in solitude. They can be made even worse by society—which is to say, by all of us in our often unconscious, habitual reactions to others in circumstances not our own. But handicaps may also be a source of devotion and energy from which society and the handicapped individual himself may benefit. This requires, however, the enlightened cooperation of society and the individual. And in the process, even in this day of movies and TV, the impersonal but inward agency of literature may be of some help.

Let me illustrate my remarks by talking about some literary personalities through the ages who have been involved with an impaired ability to walk. There are more serious handicaps, to be sure, but lameness is not a negligible thing; and perhaps I can make a few points capable of a more general application.

2

Hephaistos, the Greek god of fire—the counterpart of the Roman god Vulcan—is not the most imporant personage in Homer's *Iliad*. In fact, none of the gods are among the most important personages. Homer's interest and respect go to human beings, who after all are mortal, and risk something real when they risk their lives. Hephaistos, however, inconsistent though it must seem to those who try to find Greek mythology logical, has run his risks and paid the consequences. He limps, and has to walk with golden leg supports. The reason, as he reminds Hera, queen of the gods, the wife of Zeus, is that he had earlier offended Zeus by taking Hera's part in a quarrel she had with Zeus:

> and he caught me by the foot and threw me from the magic threshhold, and all day long I dropped helpless, and about sunset I landed in Lemnos, and there was not much life left of me.

Both of Hephaistos' legs had been broken, compounding an already existing lameness.

In reminding Hera of this, Hephaistos is trying to dissuade her from arguing again with Zeus in front of all the gods. In order to establish good feeling generally, he scurries about serving nectar to the company.

> Thereafter beginning from the left he poured drinks for the other gods, dipping up from the mixing bowl the sweet nectar. But among the blessed immortals uncontrollable laughter went up as

they saw Hephaistos bustling about the palace.

Uncontrollable laughter: the Greek gods, slightly less well-mannered than their human counterparts, respond openly, brutally to the sight even of one of their own who is unable to meet their standards of grace and dignity. There is no special malice in their laughter, no special desire to *get* Hephaistos. They just think he looks funny.

But Hephaistos is not just a figure of heartless fun in the *Iliad*. Later on the goddess Thetis wishes to procure for her son, the mortal Achilles, the finest armor that can be made, and she knows that no one can forge armor like Hephaistos. "The god of the dragging footsteps" is also "the renowned smith of the strong arms." Working in his element of fire, he is matchless.

Hephaistos is more than willing to do what Thetis asks. He remembers how she saved him at the time of his birth, when his mother Hera had thrown him with lethal intent out of Olympus, the home of the gods, because he had been born lame. (Greek divinities, like Greek mortals, were willing to seek the destruction of newborn children they considered physically inferior by abandoning them to their fate. The Greek world lacked the obligatory kind of reverence for human life fostered by the Jewish and Christian traditions.) Thetis, after saving Hephaistos, had installed him as a smith in a secret forge, until such time as Hera discovered his existence and set him up in a far posher forge of her own. Hephaistos gratefully remembers Thetis' saving of him and makes for Achilles the magnificent armor in which the hero will defeat the Trojan champion, Hector. Hephaistos will also intervene at a crucial moment to save Achilles from being killed by a Trojan river god.

What Hephaistos feels when he hears the other gods laughing at him, we don't know: Homer sayeth not. Presumably Hephaistos doesn't bear a grudge, even as he seems to have forgotten what Zeus and Hera did to him in times past. The Homeric world is a stark one, where few can afford to cry over spilt milk. Even if resentment smolders inside Hephaistos, Homer's external way of treating his characters and events would not allow us to see it. Homer—if there was a poet named Homer, and if he was, as legend has it, blind—did not let his legendary blindness incline him to a special sympathy for the limping god. But he shows that Hephaistos makes himself valued for his skills.

3

Homer sees Hephaistos from the outside, impartially, and records others' reactions to him unblinkingly. But the course of Greek civilization brought an enhanced awareness of individual suffering and an enhanced sympathy for the sufferer. Sophocles, in his *Philoctetes,* shows us a man of heroic character suffering not only from an old, magically uncured wound, but also from callous neglect and mistreatment by his fellow men. According to the legend on which Sophocles drew, Philoctetes, a member of the Greek army on the way to attack Troy, was bitten in the heel by a snake. The wound stank so offensively that Philoctetes was abandoned on a desert island. Later the Greeks learned that they could not take Troy without Philoctetes' magic bow, so they returned to the island to get the bow away from him. This is where Sophocles' play begins.

Let me simplify the action a bit. Philoctetes doesn't want to part with the bow, and the Greeks are afraid to attack him. So they use guile. The young hero Neoptolemus is persuaded, against his better instincts, to fool Philoctetes into thinking he will take him back to Greece. Philoctetes trusts Neoptolemus; and when an agonizing, maddening, totally incapacitating flareup of his wound occurs, he gives Neoptolemus the bow to hold. When Philoctetes recovers, Neoptolemus won't return the bow and tells Philoctetes to rejoin the Greek army at Troy. Philoctetes is bitterly outraged at the way Neoptolemus has taken advantage of his trust. But he knows that without the bow he cannot hunt, cannot survive. He contemplates suicide. Finally Neoptolemus, ashamed, returns the bow to Philoctetes and promises to take him back to Greece.

But that's not the end. The demigod Heracles now miraculously appears and, speaking almost as Philoctetes' conscience, directs him to rejoin the Greek forces. Philoctetes obeys. He does not forgive and forget what he has suffered so much as forego any effort at revenge or escape. He must swallow his pride. The Greek society which had disowned him still has claims on him which he cannot disown. He agrees to go to Troy and help Neoptolemus take the city—which will be to their great glory. But neither glory nor the promised cure of his wound will undo his years of painful suffering and neglect.

In spite of the vividness with which Philoctetes' physical pain and incapacitation come across to us, Sophocles does not center his attention on them. They are only marginal to his concern with a clash of interests and moralities and the men involved with it. Philoctetes' disabling wound creates few problems that an unhealed argument wouldn't create. In resolving the clash, Sophocles advances an austere notion of duty which demands largemindedness at a terrible personal cost. It is a notion which can brace handicapped and unhandicapped people alike, especially when we feel that our real merits are being overlooked because of shortcomings which should elicit helpful consideration rather than heartless cruelty from others. But it makes personal suffering, a large part of the sufferer's existence, simply something to be forgotten by him.

4

I would like to talk about one more Greek literary personage, if I may call him that. The man is Epictetus, a Greek of about 90 A.D.: an inhabitant of the Roman Empire, a slave, and also a lame one. But in addition, he is a philosopher of Stoic leanings. Epictetus wrote nothing himself; his teachings have survived through the writings of his disciple Arrian.

It is justifiable, I think, to find in Epictetus' teachings a way of resigning himself to his lowly civic status, and also to his bodily impairment. Do not concern yourself, he is reported as saying, with things not in your power; direct your attention to the things within your power. What sort of thing is not within your power? Your body, property, reputation, office. What *is* within your power? Your will and desires. Your will should not be directed into the paths of ambition, but used to cultivate rational serenity within yourself. Do not blame either the gods or men for your condition. "Lameness is an impediment to the body, but not to the will." The ideally instructed man will blame neither others nor himself. He will have nothing to complain of, since he will realize "that there is nothing good or evil save in the will: and that we are not to lead events, but to follow them."

Here is a doubly handicapped man speaking: handicapped by both slavery and lameness. He has a certain passive largeness of spirit:

> Everything has two handles, the one by which it may be borne, the other by which it may not. If your brother acts unjustly, do not lay hold of the act by that handle wherein he acts unjustly, for this is the handle which cannot be borne: but lay hold of the other, that he is your brother. . . and you will lay hold of the thing by that handle by which it can be borne.

But he discourages an active orientation towards the world. And his way of coping with the body is to try to ignore it as much as possible, rather than come to terms with it. Epictetus' attitude has a certain last-resort sort of value for anyone sorely circumstanced. In less hopeless times than his, however, surely we can try for more than his high-minded defeatism.

5

The stark peremptoriness of classical literary attitudes may seem cold to those of us westerners influenced—as who isn't?—by the Judaeo-Christian tradition. Where is love and compassion in what I have talked about? Only in subordinate manifestation: in the kindness of Thetis towards the baby Hephaistos, the ultimate generosity of Neoptolemus, the limited fellow-feeling of Epictetus.

From Israel stemmed an unprecedented emphasis on an active love for one's fellows as something enjoined by a loving but demanding God. It is the rightful and fully justified claim of Job, a man God himself calls "perfect," that Job engaged in acts of charity and mercy to others: "I was eyes to the blind, and feet to the lame." But Job, even brought low by many sufferings, including painful and incapacitating boils over his body, does not think of himself as one of the handicapped. The blind and lame are people he has done good for. They exist, as it were, to be done good for, not in themselves as people with distinct identities and personal dignity. Jesus, according to the Gospelmakers, went further. He actually cured the lame and the blind, out of pity and also as a sign of his indentity as the Son of God. His curing was a merciful concession to human frailty, though, rather than his main concern. He was primarily interested in those he cured, as in other people, as possible recruits to a kingdom not of this world. Their lives strictly in terms of this world, this flesh, were *other* to his overriding concern with fulfilling his mission.

The Christian attitude of helpful sympathy for the suffering other persisted, with change, even into times when the fervor of doctrinal religion was not what it had been in ages past, into times when men's hopes for improvements in *this* world had been kindled high, in spite of the persistence of suffering, selfishness, and inequity. To illustrate which, let me take a great leap in time forward to nineteenth-century England, Charles Dickens, and Tiny Tim.

6

When we and Scrooge, in stave three of the *Christmas Carol*, first see Tiny Tim, he is being carried into the Cratchit household by his loving father. It is a natural enough thing for a father to do, to take his child on his shoulders; but Bob does not so play with any of his other five children. This underlines Tiny Tim's handicap. "Alas for Tiny Tim, he bore a little crutch and had his limbs supported by an iron frame." Exactly how helpless he is, we don't know. He is capable of washing himself and making his way back to the company on his "active little crutch." But, although Dickens does not put it this way, the boy's family seem intent on treating him as virtually totally disabled. When he comes back into the room, his youngest brother and sister escort him to the fireside; when it's time to eat, Bob will take him to the table. Can it be that in the embarrassment of not knowing exactly how to treat him, his family would rather err on the side of oversolicitousness?

What Tim thinks of all this, we don't know. He is a thoughtful boy, though. He seems aware that he is present in the story more as an eliciter of virtuous reactions in others than as a personality in his own right. He had told Bob in church that he hoped people would notice him and remember "Him who made lame beggars walk, and blind men see." Tim's principal function, though he doesn't know it, is to wangle a cry of sympathy from the invisible Scrooge and the still more invisible reader. We are never allowed to forget his fragility. Bob holds the boy's "withered little hand in his, as if he loved the child, and wished to keep him by his side, and dreaded that he might be taken from him." Even when Tim—Dickens and the family never call him that, always "*Tiny* Tim"—even when Tim becomes excited enough to beat on the table with his knife handle, Dickens relentlessly adds that he "feebly cried Hurrah!" After dinner Tim sings a song about a lost child traveling in the snow. We learn he "had a plaintive little voice, and sang it very well indeed."

And so Dickens waxes teary over the young cripple. It is better than laughing uncontrollably, but not up to investing him with some dignity of his own. Tiny Tim remains a figure of pathos seen from the outside. Dickens continues to milk our emotions with the vision of a possible Christmas Yet to Come, where the whole Cratchit family are crushed by Tim's death. He was always "patient and mild," they say. Says the author, "Spirit of Tiny Tim, thy childish essence was from God!"

It would be unfair to accuse Dickens of engaging only in sentimental gush. There is real humanitarian concern in the story. Dickens uses Tiny Tim as an extreme exhibit in an appeal for greater charity towards the less fortunate. Tim's physical handicap functions all too obviously as a symbolic deprivation. And even as there still remains at the end of *A Christmas Carol* some middle-class condescension in the way the repentent Scrooge sends the Cratchits a Christmas turkey, promises Bob a raise, and says he will talk over Bob's affairs with him, so too there remains some of the condescension of the able-bodied towards the handicapped: Scrooge becomes to Tiny Tim a "second father." The able-bodied will never fully understand the handicapped if they look on them as parents look on helpless children.

7

Robert Browning was fond of beginning poems in an abrupt and startling manner:

> My first thought was, he lied in every word,
>   That hoary cripple, with malicious eye
>   Askance to watch the working of his lie
> On mine, and mouth scarce able to afford
> Suppression of the glee, that pursed and scored
>   Its edge, at one more victim gained thereby.
>
> What else should he be set for, with his staff?
>   What, save to waylay with his lies, ensnare
>   All travelers who might find him posted there,
> And ask the road? I guessed what skull-like laugh
> Would break, what crutch 'gin write my epitaph
>   For pastime in the dirty thoroughfare,
>
> If at his counsel I should turn aside
>   Into that omimous tract which, all agree,
>   Hides the Dark Tower.

So begins Browning's poem, "Childe Roland to the Dark Tower Came." It is a very obscure poem in concern. The title tells us nothing: there are no legends of a Childe Roland. The speaker, Roland himself, also tells us nothing about why he is engaged on the mysterious quest for the Dark Tower of which he speaks, whatever it may be. He just has to go.

And at the outside he encounters the menacing figure of a "hoary cripple," to whom he imputes malignancy and deceit. The untrustworthiness of the cripple is suggested by the way he disappears when Roland momentarily turns his back on him. But Roland finds no alternative but to turn aside, "quiet as despair," into the "ominous tract" to follow the path pointed out to him by "that hateful cripple." And he proceeds on his journey through a diseased and threatening wasteland.

Browning draws in the poem on associations seemingly as old and as widespread as the human race. And this may be because he delves into the subconscious mind, which, if Jung is right, is the same in all of us. The poem came to Browning "as in a dream." And indeed the poem has a dreamlike quality, with mysterious appearances and changes of awareness. It seems as much about changing awareness as about a journey: "Burningly it came on me—This was the place." Childe Roland finally finds himself at his Dark Tower.

What concerns me here is why one of the forms in which fears of the unknown places in the soul can concretize themselves is that of a cripple—old and seemingly deceptive to boot. Seemingly the idea of being crippled is associated in the subconscious minds of all of us with uncertain menace. Is it from fear of becoming or of being crippled ourselves? Or just from fear of the unknown? Or somehow both? Again, the poem offers only the sketchiest of indications.

Perhaps it is significant that the cripple's advice *does* prove to be correct. Translated into psychological terms, this could mean that that which we find most threatening to us may nevertheless be the surest indication to us of what we must pay respectful heed to. Translated into terms appropriate for the present discussion, it could mean that by 1852, when Browning wrote the poem, decent able-bodied people were getting to the point of recognizing how their reactions to the handicapped were conditioned not just by idealized desires to be helpful, but also by unconscious fears—which must nevertheless be faced. The *other* might not prove so menacing after all.

This is almost but not quite the same thing as seeing the handicapped and the condition of being handicapped as they are. It is one thing to face one's fears, to quit projecting them onto others as menaces; it is another thing to see the handicapped as they are in themselves. And for the latter, except insofar as we are ourselves handicapped, we need to hear a handicapped person speak for himself. This brings me to Somerset Maugham and my last literary personage, Philip Carey.

8

Somerset Maugham's *Of Human Bondage* (1915) is the partly autobiographical story of how an intelligent and excruciatingly vulnerable man learns to live at peace with the clubfoot which has been the shameful central fact of his life. It is certainly the central fact of the book, although Philip Carey's life is also complicated by the early death of his parents, his clashes of will with an unsympathetic uncle, his love problems, his loss of religious faith, and his difficulties in finding a suitable occupation. Let me run rapidly through this long and complicated book, focussing on its central theme.

Because of his congenital defect, Philip feels unwanted even as a very small boy. He overhears his godmother say that his clubfoot "was such a grief to his [dead] mother." His aunt and uncle send him off to school, where the other boys make his life miserable for a while. They twist his arm until he takes off his shoe and shows them his foot; they imitate his clumsy run; they resent it when the headmaster won't cane Philip for a minor offense because "You're a new boy. And I can't cane a cripple."

The other boys come to accept his "deformity" (Maugham's word), but Philip can't. He grows

> horribly sensitive. He never ran if he could help it, because he knew it made his limp more conspicuous, and he adopted a peculiar walk. He stood still as much as he could, with his club-foot behind the other, so that it should not attract notice, and he was constantly on the look out for any reference to it. Because he could not join in the games which other boys played, their life remained strange to him; and it seemed to him there was a barrier between them and him. Sometimes they seemed to think it was his fault if he could not play football, and he was unable to make them understand. He was left a good deal to himself.

And if the boys quit picking on Philip, a sadistic master doesn't. When Philip stumbles in the middle of a translation the master shouts, "Blockhead! Blockhead! Club-footed blockhead!"

Even the well-meaning headmaster can't help causing pain when he gives Philip the best advice he can:

> "I'm afraid your choice of professions will be rather limited. You naturally can't go in for anything that required physical activity."
>
> Philip reddened to the roots of his hair, as he always did when any reference was made to his club-foot. Mr. Perkins looked at him gravely.
>
> "I wonder if you're not oversensitive about your misfortune. Has it ever struck you to thank God for it?"
>
> Philip looked up quickly. His lips tightened. He remembered how for months, trusting in what they told him, he had implored God to heal him as he had healed the leper and made the blind to see.
>
> "As long as you accept it rebelliously it can only cause you shame. But if you looked upon it as a cross that was given you to bear only because your shoulders were strong enough to bear it, a sign of God's favour, then it would be a source of happiness to you instead of misery."

The headmaster's reasoning temporarily reconciles Philip to his foot; but Philip's continuing and finally complete loss of faith deprives him of a God to believe himself favored by.

After Philip leaves school, his consciousness of his "deformity" retreats somewhat to the background. But the feelings of unworthiness it has caused make his life hard for him. He has not developed sufficient confidence in himself to trust himself, much less to know what he wants to do. Having abandoned the thought of being ordained as a clergyman, he spends a year studying in Germany. Then he drifts into and out of accounting, into and out of the life of an art student in Paris—which he readily gives up when he hears from his teacher what he fears but almost hopes to hear: that he has no talent.

He is pathetically and uncritically eager to make friends with anyone who appears to be nice to him, and this sets him up for a number of disappointments. Even after his first affair with a woman, "he felt that no woman could ever look on him without distaste." He takes up with an ugly and uncouth art student who is drawn to him, as she makes clear, because of his "deformity." She commits suicide.

So far he hasn't fallen in love himself. But he does fall helplessly in love with the anemic waitress Mildred Rogers. He finds her attractive enough to make him put up with her insolence and indifference to him. They seem even to be part of the attraction. He hardly thinks himself worthy of better. She barely tolerates his affection. He becomes desperate enough to try to play on her pity for his club-foot. But even this degrading effort fails, and she runs off with another man.

For a while he finds consolation with understanding, maternal Norah Nesbit. She pities him, but she also loves him. And with the courage of love, she ventures to speak with him about his most touchy subject:

"It's very silly of you to be so sensitive about your club-foot," she said. She saw him flush darkly, but went on. "You know, people don't think about it nearly as much as you do. They notice it the first time they see you, and then they forget about it."

He would not answer.

"You're not angry with me, are you?"

"No."

Norah's love and good sense are not for him. Mildred, jilted by her lover, comes running back to Philip, and their relationship drags its hideous way on. He abases himself for her in many ways, even funding a weekend for her with her latest lover, his friend Griffiths. But he finally becomes disenchanted with her. Realizing she has lost her hold on him, she hurls at him the thing she knows will hurt him the most: the word "cripple!"

But by this stage in his life, Philip is becoming strong enough to accept his handicap. He has started studying to be a doctor, and the impartiality of medical training helps him to regard physical problems dispassionately. He is offended when he is asked to bare his foot to show other medical students. But he realizes that his instructor isn't malicious; and later, he is able to bear up without flinching at references to his foot. And he becomes a capable physician, and is recognized as such.

Finally—I have left out much—Philip attains peace. He has found a woman he feels able to propose to.

And thinking back over the long pilgrimage of his past he accepted it joyfully. He accepted the deformity which had made life so hard for him; he knew also that it had warped his character, but now he saw also that by reason of it he had acquired that power of introspection which had given him so much delight. Without it he would never have had his keen appreciation of beauty, his passion for art and literature, and his interest in the varied spectacle of life. The ridicule and the contempt which had so often been heaped upon him had turned his mind inward and called forth those flowers which he felt would never lose their fragrance. Then he saw that the normal was the rarest thing in the world. Everyone had some defect of body or of mind: he thought of all the people he had known, (the whole world was like a sick-house, and there was no rhyme or reason for it,) he saw a long procession, deformed in body and warped in mind, some with illness of the flesh, weak hearts or weak lungs, and some with illness of the spirit, languor of will or a craving for liquor. At this moment he could feel a holy compassion for them all. They were the helpless instruments of blind chance. He could pardon Griffiths for his treachery and Mildred for the pain she had caused him. They could not help themselves. The only reasonable thing was to accept the good of men and be patient with their faults. The words of the dying God crossed his memory:

Forgive them, for they know not what they do.

9

Philip Carey's story is a painful one, more painful maybe than it had to be. It must have been painful to write. It is not totally free of self-disgust and self-pity. But I feel at the end that Philip Carey—like his creator—has earned his right to some happiness. No more than Hephaistos, the lame blacksmith, did he let his handicap pronounce the last word on him. But now, so to speak, we know how Hephaistos felt. There will surely be other handicapped wordsmiths, not necessarily handicapped in Maugham's way, who will have more to tell us twentieth-century readers of what their lives are like. And we can all be the richer for it.

WORKS CITED

Browning, Robert. "Childe Roland to the Dark Tower Came." 1855; rpt
The Shorter Poems of Robert Browning, ed. William Clyde De Vane.
New York: Appleton-Century Crofts, 1934.

Defoe, Daniel. *Robinson Crusoe.* 1720; rpt. New York: Macmillan, 1962.

Dickens, Charles. *A Christmas Carol.* 1843; rpt. New York: Dutton, 1972.

Epictetus. *Discourses.* Cambridge: Harvard University Press.

Homer, *The Iliad.* trans. R. Lattimore. Chicago: Univ. Chicago, 1951.

Hood, Thomas. "Faithless Nelly Gray." *Selected Poems of Thomas Hood,* ed.
John Clubbe. Cambridge: Harvard Univ. Pr., 1970.

Irving, Washington. *Knickerbocker's History of New York.* Ed. Anne C.
Moore. New York: Ungar, 1959.

Maugham, Somerset. *Of Human Bondage.* 1915; rpt. New York: Penguin,
1978.

Melville, Herman, *Moby Dick.* 1851; rpt. New York: Abrams, 1976.

Sophocles. "Philoctetes." *Tragedies.* 2 vols. Cambridge: Harvard Univ. Press.

Stevenson, Robert Louis. *Treasure Island.* 1883; rpt. New York: Macmillan,
1963.

LITERARY IMAGES
AS STEREOTYPES
by Bruce Dearing

Readers concerned with images of disability may be familiar with the assertion that the poet is the unacknowledged legislator of mankind, and another one in which a poet said, "If I may write your songs, I care not who may write your laws." I do not quite believe this; nevertheless there is something in the idea. Literature and the other arts are influential expressions of climates of opinion and of popular attitudes and perceptions within a culture. They are very strong agents in the institutionalization and perpetuation of ideas and feelings, and are therefore worthy of study. Accordingly, we need to take the first step of identifying stereotypical images of disability in literature.

As a case in point, what may be the single most widely recognized literary character with a handicapping condition is Shakespeare's King Richard III. His characterization of Richard epitomizes certain attitudes in Renaissance England which have persisted to our own time. The continuing currency of that symbol has made it powerfully influential. Even people who have never read Shakespeare or seen the play are likely to know something about the monster Richard III. There is a fascinating book about him called *Daughter of Time* (from the proverb "Truth is the daughter of time") by the detective story writer Josephine Tey. She uses as a fictional framework for rediscovering some truths about the historical Richard III. A temporarily hospitalized detective, while recuperating, becomes interested in reconstructing the history of the last Plantagenet king, Richard III. In the process he rediscovers what has been periodically relearned but quickly forgotten because of the power of Shakespeare's institutionalized symbol.

The detective again uncovers the fact that Richard III was an able soldier, a skillful politican and a capable monarch, who in the two short troubled years of his reign still managed to enact a number of excellent laws still on the books in modern England. Only a man of unusual physical strength and intellectual power could have achieved the career objective history concedes him. The myth, of course, is that Richard was evil incarnate, that he was a cruel, unfeeling villain, a disastrous and destructive leader and a grotesque hunchback born with a full set of sharp teeth. He was vilified as a hunchback toad, a venomous spider, and a savage wild boar (his crest, emblazoned on his shield, was the figure of a boar). The truth seems to be that he had one shoulder a little higher than the other, largely because of an overdeveloped sword arm; he personally wielded the heavy weapons of the period in his many military campaigns as the principal field general of his brother King Edward IV. His contemporary portraits reveal a handsome, somewhat ascetic countenance. The explanation for this striking discrepancy between myth and fact is simple enough. Shakespeare's play was Tudor political propaganda within the dramatic tradition of the revenge play and the tragedy of blood following Marlowe.

Richard III was the last of the Plantagenet dynasty and the last English King with an unquestioned and unqualified claim to the throne. He was killed at Bosworth Field defending his throne against Queen Elizabeth's grandfather Henry Tudor, whose claim to the title was very tenuous indeed. It was based upon descent through an illegitimate line of the progeny of John of Gaunt and depended on a number of shaky legalisms. Shakespeare wrote his historical plays, among other things, as a Tudor apologist. He was following the account of Polydore Virgil, official historiographer to Henry VII, and another account by Thomas Morton, Bishop of Ely and one of the successful rebels against Richard.

The significance for purposes of our enquiry is that Shakespeare used physical deformity as a ready device to mirror and symbolize mental and spiritual ugliness. Disfigurement is thus simultaneously projected as cause, effect, and symbol of wicked behavior. In Act V, Richard is addressed by the parade of ghosts that invade his tent before the battle at Bosworth to chant a litany: "You are God's enemy, despair and die!" Shakespeare's art always subtlized and humanized to some degree; as dramatist he was apparently incapable of drawing a truly one-dimensional character. One thinks for example, of Shylock as a muted or slightly ameliorated version of anti-semitism in Elizabethan England. Shylock is allowed to ask movingly: "Has not a Jew eyes?" "If you prick us, do we not bleed? If you poison us, do we not die?" Though Richard has fleeting moments of self-justification in the play, he is forever etched in the popular imagination as a mis-shapen monster of evil power. The first scene opens with this revealing soliloquy:

> But I, that am not shap'd for sportive tricks,
> Nor made to court an amorous looking-glass;
> I, that am rudely stamp'd, and want love's majesty
> To strut before a wanton ambling nymph;
> I, that am curtail'd of this fair proportion,
> Cheated of feature by dissembling nature,
> Deform'd, unfinish'd, sent before my time
> Into this breathing world, scarce half made up,
> And that so lamely and unfashionable
> That dogs bark at me as I halt by them;
> Why, I, in this weak piping time of peace,
> Have no delight to pass away the time,
> Unless to see my shadow in the sun
> And descant on mine own deformity.
> And therefore, since I cannot prove a lover
> To entertain these fair well-spoken days,

I am determined to prove a villain
And hate the idle pleasures of these days,
Plots have I laid, inductions dangerous,
By drunken prophecies, libels, and dreams...

(Act I, Scene I)

It is odd and ironic that by contrast another Richard Plantagenet, Richard I, who has survived in myth as the heroic Crusader King, the understanding friend of Robin Hood, and the virtuous foil to his brother the evil King John, was historically one of the worst of English Kings. He had very little capacity for or interest in governing. He apparently was a blood-thirsty warrior who was never really happy except when he was in the field. He had the advantage of being over six feet tall at a time when most knights were scarcely more than five feet tall, and he truly enjoyed beheading Saracens. He was also almost surely homosexual, and though that orientation is not in our time regarded as necessarily an illness or an evil, it would have been through much of English history. His portrait in Goldman's *The Lion in Winter* is historically well-founded in suggesting his treacherous propensities. The striking difference between the usual perceptions of the muscular, well-formed, physically strong Richard I and the slightly malformed Richard III are instructive. But Richard III is merely one of many cases of prejudice by impairment which need to be identified.

There are several possible ways of organizing an inquiry into the workings of the literary imaginzation as they relate to the issues of physical handicaps. We could proceed historically or typologically. An historical approach could begin with ancient Greek myths of Tiresias, the androgynous and perhaps hermaphroditic seer; the lame, later blinded and consistently unlucky Oedipus Rex; the lame and ridiculed Greek Hephaestos or Roman Vulcan; and the outcast swamp monster Grendel, whom Beowulf quite literally disarmed. All of these mythic and somewhat monstrous figures are clearly anthropomorphic projections of human abilities and disabilities. One could trace such symbols to the diminished present in a work like Ken Kesey's *One Flew Over the Cuckoo's Nest,* presenting the mental hospital as a microcosm of the world outside. The drama culminates in the lobotomization of the amiable misfit McMurphy by his enemy Big Nurse Ratched and the tyrannous system she represents, and his death at the hands of his friend, the supposedly paranoid native American, Chief Bromden. Or, we could look at Dr. Strangelove as a confluence of popular themes of the mad scientist, the super-human, *cum* sub-human, *cum* non-human Hun and the sinister, vengeful, over-compensating paraplegic.

Another way of organizing these various literary types is with a typology of the characteristics attitudes toward those with handicapping conditions. One such typology has been outlined by Ellen Barnes. She points out that all such attitudes are inter-actional, and cites as conventional perceptions that:

1. A handicap is a sickness, that is something to be fixed, an abnormality to be corrected.

2. Handicapped people are sub-human, that is, inferior, devalued, lesser persons.

3. An impaired person is a menace, a danger to himself, to others and to society.

4. A handicapped person is a "holy innoncent" with a special grace, a unique protection or immunity invoked as a counterpoise to physical or psychic disadvantage.

5. A handicapped person is an appropriate object of pity and often grudging charity, a personal and social burden to be dealt with by the unimpaired through distancing and withholding of self.

With rare exceptions literary images will fit into one or another, or a combination of these essentially negative categories.

A third approach, a modification of which I shall follow, is a typology of literary characters and attitudes towards them according to specific handicapping conditions such as blindness, deafness, epilepsy, cerebral palsy, Down's syndrome, orthopedic problems, and so forth. Literary characters defined in this way tend to be presented from the outside as antagonists rather than from the inside as protagonists, and with a consistently negative valence, in spite of some ambiguously positive elements and some extremely rare instances of genuine celebration of the humanity, strength and capacity which is at least as characteristic of the handicapped as of so-styled "normal" counterparts. Let us briefly examine a few of these proposed categories.

AMPUTATION. Captain Hook of *Peter Pan,* the pirate Long John Silver of *Treasure Island,* and Captain Ahab of Melville's *Moby Dick* are all figures of demonic power and monomoniacal intensity. (Even the saccharin in *Peter Pan* cannot entirely obscrue the underlying fear and loathing). Their mutilation sets them apart from ordinary heroes and villains, and while one may feel awe or grudging admiration, these are not figures to inspire affection or emulation. Peter Stuyvesant, General Herkimer, Horatio, Lord Nelson, Douglas Bader, and other stalwart military figures are historical rather than literary, and despite the heroic attributes assigned to them, they are endowed with positive values primarily within the contexts of warfare and celebration of empire.

Wilfred Owen offers a poignant insight into the devaluation of disabled veterans in peacetime. He knew intimately wherof he spoke. He himself, a few months after he wrote the following poem, was a casualty of World War I. The poem is entitled "Disabled":

He sat in a wheeled chair, waiting for dark,
And shivered in his ghastly suit of grey,
Legless, sewn short at elbow. Through the park
Voices of boys rang saddening like a hymn,
Voices of play and pleasures after day,
Till gathering sleep had mothered them from him.
About this time Town used to swing so gay
When glow-lamps budded in the light blue trees,
And girls glanced lovelier as the air grew dim,—

In the old times, before he threw away his knees.
Now he will never feel again how slim
Girls' waists are, or how warm their subtle hands;
All of them touch him like some queer disease.

                    *   *   *

Some cheered him home, but not as crowds cheer Goal.
Only a solemn man who brought him fruits
Thanked him; and then inquired about his soul.
Now he will spend a few sick years in Institutes,
And do what things the rules consider wise,
And take whatever pity they may dole,
Tonight he noticed how the women's eyes
Passed from him to the strong men that were whole.
How cold and late it is! Why don't they come
And put him into bed? Why don't they come?

Other images of amputees include Porgy, of Gershwins' popular opera *Porgy and Bess* (novel by D. Heyward), who is both a folk hero and an original creation, as he triumphs over the debasement of his leglessness and of his socioeconomic status. Those with largely invisible and well-compensated injuries may be portrayed most sympathetically. Take for example, Alan Quatermain, the hero of several H. Rider Haggard novels, whose cork leg is only a minor impediment, and the characters portrayed in films by the late Herbert Marshall, whose distinctive walk subtly acknowledge a similar prosthesis for a war wound. Thorton Wilder invented a quadruple amputee, a totally reclusive retired Legion Commander, to serve as wise counselor to Julius Caesar. In a macabre invention a science fiction writer has imagined a world in grotesque reversal and perhaps satiric illumination of our present uneasy male-dominant society. In that unsettling fiction (at least I find it unsettling) all males are quadruple amputees maintained as pampered pets by dominant, intrepid women.

PARAPLEGIA. Seen externally only, Dr. Strangelove is a paraplegic figure of power and menace. Clifford Chatterly of D.H. Lawrence's *Lady Chatterly's Lover,* is portrayed as impotent, dependent, cold, and emotionally anaesthetized. He is irritating and tiresome, rather than sympathetic—simply somebody to be got out of the way, so that Lady Chatterly can live more fully with her game-keeper lover, Mellors. The wheelchair-borne old man of Katherine Ann Porter's *Ship of Fools* is principally a burden, a tyrannous demanding old hulk without any redeeming humanity, and again seen from outside.

Among positive images, Raymond Burr's T.V. character, Ironside, is portrayed as a kind of supercop, perhaps in the tradition of blind, obese or otherwise necessarily restricted characters capable of uncommon concentration. (For example, Sherlock Holmes' older, smarter, fatter brother, Mycroft, or Nero Wolfe, both of whom solved problems without straying outside their secluded homes.) In a contemporary novel by Wilfred Sheed, *People Will Always Be Kind,* Brian Casey emerges initially as a courageous fighter who overcomes the limitations imposed by polio to become first a campus leader and then a successful politican. But by the end of the book he is portrayed essentially from the outside, as revengeful and arrogant, bent on exacting obedience from subordinates on their knees before his wheelchair. He savors compensatory power through humiliating other people and bending them to his will.

MENTAL RETARDATION. In *Down's Syndrome* of mental retardation we may note a significant semantic consideration in which the older term "mongoloid" or "monogloid child" is vulgarized into "Mongolian idiot." The eye folds and the round face characteristic of the physical appearance of such children get generalized into the inscrutability, unreachability, and threatening strangeness of the "yellow peril" from the East. Such an image could not survive direct acquaintance with genuine Down's syndrome children, many of whom are remarkedly loving and lovable. I have learned from association with the Medical Center that most physicians who work with such children become their champions and advocates, rather than their devaluators.

In Steinbeck's *Of Mice and Men* (the title is from Burns' poem "The best laid plans o' mice and men/ fu' often gang aglee/ and leave us 'naught but grief and pain/ for promised joy"), Lenny is partly the holy innocent. Essentially a naive child in a powerful adult body, he does not know his own strength. Lacking sophisticated control when he tries to pet any small appealing creature, he inevitably crushes it. When ultimately he kills a woman toward whom he is trying to express affection, he is subjected to euthanasia by his friend to keep him from falling into the hands of uncomprehending and hostile authorities. In a way his fate parallels that of McMurphy, who is smothered by his friend, Chief Bromden, after he has been reduced by vengeful lobotomization to what is called a "vegetable."

Another case is that of Boo Radley in Harper Lee's *To Kill a Mockingbird*. His father is ashamed of him, keeps him hidden away, tries to correct for him, and blocks up the hollow tree which has served as a message center between the retarded boy-man and his accepting young friends next door. Boo Radley becomes an ambiguous hero when he kills the lawless Bob Ewell in protecting the children of his generous neighbor, and is in turn protected from prosecution by a sympathetic sheriff and lawyer in deference to his disabilities. One of the rescued children and her lawyer father agree that it would be as tasteless and needlessly destructive to drag the shy man into the pitiless spotlight of a lurid courtroom trial, as it would be to kill a mockingbird.

Ring Lardner's "Haircut" is one of the most troubling of short stories. The dramatic occasion is one in which an ignorant, bigoted barber progressively reveals to his captive client and the reader the circumstantial evidence of a murder by an abused brain-injured boy of an entirely cruel and destructive local practical joker, generally admired for his "machismo." It seems to me significant that both these figures, Boo Radley and the brain-injured boy in "Haircut" achieve recognition as valuable persons only through homicide.

Billy, the retarded boy in "The Last Picture Show," is an inoffensive victim of good-natured and well-meaning horseplay by boys who mean to be friendly to him, and is devalued in his death when run down by a truck while he is bemusedly sweeping the roadway with a broom. The townspeople are more irritated with Billy for getting in the way of the truck than they are at the unfeeling truck driver for having run him down. Only his luckless, partially blinded friend Sonny really mourns his loss.

EPILEPSY. There seems to be little literary attention given to epilepsy. Even though Dostoevsky, one of the most psychologically sophisticated of novelists, was himself an epileptic, and presents two of his characters, Prince Myshkin in Dostoevsky's *The Idiot* and Smerdyakof in his *Brothers Karamazov* as epileptics, he does not focus on the illness. In *The Idiot*, Prince Myshkin is a kind of holy innocent, childishly trusting, naive, simple, kindly, affectionate, easily exploited, but too unworldly to survive in normal society. He retreats to an asylum to escape painful experiences in the harsh world of reality. By contrast, Smerdyakof is mad, evil, and manipulative. He is literally a murderous bastard, a parricide whose three legitimate siblings also have some destructive tendencies.

The biblical King Saul is supposed to have suffered from seizures of some kind, perhaps epileptic, which may account in some part for his behavior towards David. Julius Caesar was well recognized as suffering from the ''falling sickness,'' which was seen both as a mark of genius and favor of the gods, and also as perhaps a fatal weakness in a leader, especially in the eyes of a literalist like Shakespeare's Cassius.

LAMENESS. There is a considerable literature of lameness. Hephaestos (the Roman Vulcan), the god of smiths and fire, was the butt of jokes among his fellow gods; the principal myth in which he figures concerns the occasion in which his wife Aphrodite (Venus) deceived him with Ares (Mars), the god of war. The vengeful cuckold, by devising a very ingenious net, was able to capture the lovers *in flagrante delictu* and got perhaps an intermediate laugh but hardly the last laugh. Most onlookers envied and sympathized with Ares rather than with Hephaestos. In an obscure Elizabethan version of another powerful myth, called ''Swellfoot the Tyrant,'' Oedipus Rex was a marvelous complex of ironies that not only Sophocles but Freud could seize upon to illuminate the human condition. Oedipus was originally exposed to die as a defective infant with an orthopedic problem—perhaps a club foot. He survived by being rescued by a stranger, grew to manhood without knowing his true origins, and endured a series of misfortunes including meeting and quarreling with his natural father, becoming an unwitting parricide, and compounding the error in an incestuous marriage with his natural mother. These luckless crimes precipitated a series of plagues on Thebes which, when he discovered himself as the offender, caused Oedipus to blind and exile himself in expiation.

Significantly he gained his initial power by solving the riddle of the Sphinx: ''What goes on four legs in the morning, two legs at noon three legs in the evening?'' The answer of course is *man,* passing from the helplessness of the crawling infant through the strength of adulthood to the helplessness and weakness of old age, leaning on a staff. One is reminded of the misquotation of

Ecclesiastes by Willie Stark in Robert Penn Warren's novel *All the King's Men*, when he says "Man is for a little time and full of trouble. He passes from the stink of the didie to the stench of the shroud and there is no health in him."

In Somerset Maugham's *Of Human Bondage*, Philip Carey is one of the few examples of an introspective lame protagonist. Maugham was a trained physician drawing upon clinical knowledge in creating a character who was presented to my student generation as a key to understanding the problem of adolescence and early maturity. Philip Carey had a club foot which was presumably responsible for an abnormal sensitivity and self-depreciation, and for his neurotic difficulty in freeing himself from the shallow, unfeeling, thoroughly exploitative waitress and prostitute, Mildred. There are other familiar examples of pathetic lame children, of whom we probably know best Dickens' Tiny Tim and Jenny Wren. Giancarlo Menotti managed a much more insightful and favorable portrait of a lame child in *Amahl and the Night Visitors,* but it is still essentially sentimental. In Tennessee Williams' "The Glass Menagerie," Tom remembers his sister Laura as a sweet but pathetic recluse limited by a orthopedic problem. In the twilight zone between fantasy and real life, the lameness of the poet Byron, compensated by his handsome face, prowess in swimming, and creative genius, seems to have enhanced rather than diminished his romantic interest.

BLINDNESS. When we turn to blindness in literature, Teiresias the androgynous blind seer comes immediately to mind. Oedipus the King punished himself by blinding. Shakespeare's King Lear was symbolically blind as well as temporarily deranged and one of the other principal characters in the play, Gloucester, was literally blinded. The entire play is full of analyses of the problems of misperception, inappropriate interpretation, and self deceit. Thick glasses or dark sun glasses are often used as symbols of menance, perhaps because the eyes in popular imagination are indeed windows of the soul. If the eyes of an encountered person are masked or concealed, he becomes in some way menacing. The sharpshooting guard in the film "Cool Hand Luke" is a striking case in point. Another example would be the blind hit men in Duerrenmatt's play "The Visit." Blind Pew in Stevenson's *Treasure Island* is a terrifying nemesis, who despite his blindness, traces down and kills people who have been fingered by the Pirate organization. Dumas has a painfully poignant short story about the gratuitous cruelty to a harmless blind man by people who are otherwise kindly.

FACIAL DISFIGUREMENT. This seems to evoke more fear and horror than most other disabilities. For example, in *The Phanton of the Opera,* Lon Chaney, the first great makeup artist, plays the role of a kindly, sensitive person who had been horribly scarred by acid burns and had consequently retreated completely from the world, taking refuge in the opera house where he could only relate to others by occasional terrifying appearances. My own most vivid recollection of youthful reading is not Shakespeare or Grimm's Fairy Tales, but a serial story in *The American Boy* about "Skull Face the Terrible," an American Indian who had been fearfully wounded by the stroke of a bear's paw, stripping much of the flesh from his face. While he was powerful and intrepid and not initially evil, he became a figure of terror to a whole frontier region where he operated as an outcast much like Grendel. A Saturday afternoon movie serial I remember with most chilling vividness was one called "Still Face." The principal character had been wounded in World War I and had lost any capacity to show expression. Behind his absolutely immobile face he was completely unreadable and unreachable. Despite experience with many later horror movies, this was the one I remember as most frightening and distressing.

Steven Crane wrote a very distressing short story called "The Monster" which features Henry Johnson, a good-spirited servant who is facially disfigured by an acid explosion while rescuing the son of his physician employer during a terrible fire. The upshot is that while the physician is able to save the servant's life, it is at the expense of the social destruction of the physician, his wife, his children, and the monster himself because they are all completely rejected by neighbors and associates. The local judge tells him, "This is your own fault. That man should be dead; you resurrected him and therefore he has become your nemesis."

Readers of comic strips will recall the parade of villains in Dick Tracy, most of whom have severe facial abnormalities: Prune face, whose face is severely wrinkled and rumpled; Half and Half, who has a handsome right side and a disfigured left side, and so on. Viewers of the late movies may have seen in reruns the lepers in *Ben Hur*. Their greatest concern was hiding their ravaged faces, but the mother and daughter became symbols of the power of the Christ when they were healed and restored to their former beauty, able to return to normal society after having been totally rejected and cruelly exiled.

DEAFNESS. This disability seems generally to be sympathetically portrayed. One may hazard the guess that one of the reasons that deafness is so little associated with evil and meance is that it is perhaps least threatening to others. There is no accompanying oddity of appearance, especially if the deaf person also does not speak (though in speaking there may be a voice tone unheard by the speaker but troublesome to the uninstructed). Presumably there is neither fear of contagion, nor any demeaning association in deafness. It is probably easier for most "normal" people to empathize with deaf persons and to recognize the nature of their isolation and the cutting off of communication, than with people suffering different kinds of handicapping conditions. Mark Twain, in *The Adventures of Huckleberry Finn*, offers a very moving account by the slave Jim of his discovery that his own unresponsive daughter was unfortunately deaf and not culpably defiant—unable to hear the commands her father had been punishing her for disobeying. I had to give up reading the passage to literature classes because I found it moved me to tears, and I confess even now to becoming choked up even thinking about it. Presumably this has something to do with parenting, and with the idea of being unintentionally unfeeling in misreading a condition which deserves not censure but understanding and empathy.

In John Betjeman's "Portrait of a Deaf Man," the poet describes the life of a man who loved birds even though he couldn't hear them, and expresses his regret that he was never able really to communicate with the deaf man. The final stanza reads: "And when he could not hear me speak/He smiled and looked so wise/That now I do not like to think/Of maggots in his eyes." John Singer in Carson McCullers' *The Heart Is a Lonely Hunter* is a deaf mute driven to suicide despite his "understanding friends" who never really comprehend his needs or his gifts. When he is unable to save a friend from dying in the hospital, he can no longer stand to live in a world that thinks it is being understanding and kind to him. Quasimodo, *The Hunchback of Notre Dame*, is deaf as well as disfigured. In Victor Hugo's fiction he is initially presented as a figure of fun, playfully crowned as a comic Pope. He is nevertheless full of yearnings for relationships with the beautiful heroine and the handsome hero, and is a generally sympathetic rather than a contemptuously dismissed figure.

SPEECH DISORDERS. Among those suffering from speech disorders we may think of the character Billy Bibbit in Ken Kesey's *One Flew Over the Cuckoo's Nest.* Billy is driven to suicide by "Big Nurse Rached" after his stammering shyness, his terror of his domineering mother, and his sexual anxiety have been to some extent relieved through the rude ministrations of his institutionalized friends through arranging an encounter with a prostitute. Sugar Boy, in Robert Penn Warren's *All the King's Men,* is an emotionally bottled up, stammering bodyguard and chauffeur who takes out his fury in skillful but hazardous driving. There is a long tradition of subliterary humor poking fun at the speech of those afflicted by stammering, hare lip, cleft palate, or dyslexia. Most of us have heard many such jokes and witticisms at the expense of sufferers and many of us have only recently given up laughing at them or repeating them, as consciousness has belatedly been raised. The labored or blurred speech of the cerebral palsied has been far too often misconstrued as indicating mental incapacity. Such mistakes open the way for appalling insensitivity and unitentional cruelty by those who assume they are relating to dim-witted and childish handicapped persons, rather than to persons with unimpaired intelligences and acute sensitivities very like their own.

OBESITY. We may briefly note the irony that obesity seems to be surprisingly strongly disapproved in our generally overweight culture. Recent studies, particularly relating to young children, of the hierarchy of disabilities from least threatening to most threatening or most favored to least favored, systematically reveal obesity as the most devaluating of disabilities, ranking well beyond others one might have projected as more seriously devaluing. In literature, however, fat people tend to be stereotyped as full of jollity (Mr. Pickwick, Friar Tuck, Santa Claus) despite some dark portraits such as the sinister fat boy in Dickens' *Pickwick Papers* and a whole set of smoothly villainous characters played in the movies by Sidney Greenstreet.

FANTASY MONSTERS. Contemporary children seem to be fascinated by monsters as presented on T.V. and in comic strips. The current crop of mythic monsters are worth examination. Monsters imagined by authors and script-writers still tend to be anthropomorphic projections of certain human characteristics. In ancient tradition they were rarely mere genetic mutations or accidents of birth involving physical anomalies, and were not always associated with large size, menacing uncontrollability and physical invulnerability as they seem now to be. They have always tended to be human, subhuman, superhuman or humanoid. The Minotaur, for example, was half man and half bull, a centaur—part horse, a satyr—part goat, a mermaid—part woman and "all fish below the thighs." Fell Grendel was some sort of swamp spirit, reptilian and cannibalistic. The current comic strip heroes from Superman to Spiderman and antagonists such as Dr. Octopus, Dr. Doom, are primarily exaggerated anthropoid figures.

Perhaps the most impressive continuing symbols of monstrous disability continue to be Frankenstein's monster and Count Dracula. Both are surely associated with death taboos. The vampire is perhaps the ultimate in dependence, because he has not only envious malice but a desperate need for drinking the blood of living creatures in order to maintain his own precarious existence. However, the more significant figure would appear to be Frankenstein's monster. There is striking discontinuity between the first literary conception and the Boris Karloff movie version which has largely determined modern ideas of monsterhood. Mary Wolstonecroft Shelley, wife of the poet, in her original novel described the "daemon" first as a handsome and morally innocent creature who was only later degraded and corrupted by ugly civilization in which he had to make his difficult way. He was a version of the "noble savage" postulated by Rousseau. I think it must say something about our generation and our literary needs that when this story came to the screen, Boris Karloff portrayed the monster as a debased caricature of normal humanity, a patchwork of cadavers with bolts coming out of his neck and multiple surgical sutures everywhere in evidence. Worst of all, he has a criminal brain, through an error of the deformed servant Igor, who had dropped the normal brain stolen from an Anatomy Laboratory, and was forced to substitute an abnormal one. The monster is inarticulate. He moves with painful clumsiness. He has rudimentary intelligence and emotions, but at the same time uncontrolled power and potential for savagery. He is some ways a terrifyingly dehumanized parallel to Steinbeck's Lenny. The monster is nearly invulnerable; he is in a way unkillable because he is already dead. He proves to be controllable only by threatening with torches, and ultimately he is incinerated.

In summary, it would seem that images of handicapping conditions are portrayed and perpetuated through literary and sub-literary characters in identifiable patterns. First, they are generally negative, defensive, fearful, hostile, rationalizing. Second, they seem to be observed from outside. The characters are rarely protagonists. They are occasionally impressive antagonists, such as Grendel, Dracula and Frankenstein's creation. However, handicapped people more often play minor supporting roles as mere items in the environments of the principal characters. Third, even when the portrayal is multi-dimensional and sympathetic, there still tends to be a focus upon the handicapped person's helplessness, victimization, loneliness, isolation, and sadness. Rarely is there a positive celebration of strength, courage, achievement, ingenious adaptation or capable compensation. In non-fiction affirmative biographies of Helen Keller and others who have triumphed over disability may help to restore a balance; but stereotypes are heavily weighted toward the negative.

Even in Paul Gallico's *The Snow Goose,* the lonely, sensitive hunchbacked fisherman achieves full acceptance as a human peer only at the expense of his life through heroic exploits in his sailboat during the British evacuation of Dunquerque. This moving, but essentially sentimental, story would have quite other overtones had the fisherman returned in triumph to marry the no less lonely girl with whom he diffidently shared the rehabilitation of the heavily symbolic wounded snow goose. Paraplegic Brian Casey in Sheed's novel *People Will Always Be Kind,* achieved his political power at the expense of becoming ruthless, cyncial, and exploitative. Tiny Tim is pathetic and fragile, a cardboard valentine rather than a fully realized literary character. Lenny, as noted, had to be destroyed to be saved. We may concede with a wince that sentimental indulgence is no more appropriate or helpful than mere indifference or jeering hostility.

Finally, there is ample evidence of the embarrassment, uncertainty, and uneasiness of society attempting to relate to handicapped persons in full and accepting common humanity. The most usual coping, distancing and insulating devices and mechanisms are, in many ways, inadequate and inappropriate to the situation. One familiar device is devaluation by infantilization: for examples, by shouting or using childish language in talking to mature and sentient handicapped persons, or pushing a sightless person ahead of oneself, rather than thoughtfully leading with a companion at one's elbow. Sentimental pity, uninvolved charity and general depersonalization are equally unwelcome. There is a great deal of anxiety-reducing humor (by no means confined to children) in relating to people with disabilities—that is, reducing the anxiety of those who use such humor as a weapon in taunting, ridiculing, and other verbal aggression.

There is a deplorable history of exploitation, social and economic, of handicapped people. Circus freaks, such as the "Elephant Man" of Victorian times (rescued finally by an understanding physician who saw a person behind the grotesque disfigurement of the boy on exhibition) are classic examples of exploitation. The travelling carnivals I remember from fifty years algo always featured a "Half-man, Half-woman" alongside the fat lady, the giant and the midget. For centuries the role of the jester and the licensed fool have been played by midgets, hunchbacks, or other physically impaired but witty persons; presumably their cloak of strangeness legitimized the uncomfortable jokes and satiric depreciations which would not otherwise have been permitted in the solemnity and threatening political ambiance of the royal court.

In our time, among the major exploitations are many elements of the arrangements for institutionalization of handicapped persons. Too often it appears that the presumed beneficiaries are rather less accommodated than the unimpaired who gain by employment, building construction and maintenance, and other contributions to a profit making economy. Advocacy groups have of late been pointing out some of the disturbing similarities between prisons and institutional "Homes" for the elderly, the mentally disturbed, and those with other handicapping conditions.

Another familiar form of depersonalization is the process of mythologization—the identification of handicapped people with sin and punishment ("they must somehow deserve their distress"); with the holy innocent ("We don't have to worry about them because God looks after fools and drunkards"); or the subhuman ("They neither need nor require our notice"); or the object of fear ("It is right to keep our distance because they might harm us."). More appropriate mechanisms should develop from understanding and appreciation founded upon genuine empathy and compassion. Not pity, but ungrudging acceptance of vulnerable fellow mortals within the human condition is a reasonable goal. We all require recognition of the commonality behind apparent differences, and of the common needs, aspirations and capacities that permit accepting and even celebrating, rather than devaluating diversity of personality and physique. An easy and familiar association seems to be helpful in correcting for prejudices of this kind. We can admire Dorothy Parker's succinct observation: "For me, familiarity does not breed contempt, only more familiarity." Doubtless she was speaking of another kind of interpersonal relation; nevertheless she illuminates the way in which we relate to people we have come to know, as against the way in which we deal with strangers.

The most difficult problem, of course, is to devise specific strategies to develop creative and appropriate coping mechanisms, and to modify one's own life style as he enters the health professions, the teaching profession, social work, or any other supportive employment. One promising approach is consciousness raising—simply bringing into awareness and recognition, and then challenging stereotypes. Before I prepared this essay, I was largely unaware of the disturbing consistency of negative portrayal of disability in literature. Clearly we need more open discussion and more vigorous advocacy of humane treatment for all persons. Those concerned with "handicapism" may find useful analogies in parallel campaigns against racism and sexism, in efforts to achieve prison reform, and an effort now gathering momentum in breaking the taboo upon acknowledgement of death as a fact of life. Perhaps these liberating principles represent ideas whose time has come, on strong evidence that the climate regarding issues of this kind has changed markedly within the last decade.

One practical approach is the training of teachers and opinion leaders. There is a need and a capacity for the production and selection of teaching materials. For example, Alex Haley's *Roots,* with its phenomenal success both as a book and as a television special, has been powerfully influential on attitudes. For once, mass media were effectively used in raising the consciousness of millions of Americans to a part of our history usually only vaguely and abstractly considered. We can hope that this massive common experience may permanently change the attitudes of many citizens toward the relationship between Black and White Americans.

Ms. Magazine has an engaging feature presenting children's stories with heroines rather than heros. Charlotte Pomerantz among others has published some brilliant children's stories about intelligent princesses rather than shrewd and capable little tailors or All-American boys, or Mickey-Mouse male figures. Newly available children's literature, though it cannot as yet compete with the popularity of monster movies and traditional books like *Treasure Island*, has high potential. A thick bibliography sponsored by the Division for Handicapped Children, New York State Education Department, inlcudes some hundreds of books appropriate for developing helpful and healthy attitudes of teachers and pupils alike toward the variety of human circumstance, including handicapping conditions.

It seems important to recognize the special role of health care personnel; whether physicians, nurses, physical therapists, or other, as an essential first line of support. We in the medical community need to be acutely and with sophistication aware of our own attitudes and to be intimately in touch with our own feelings if we are to be truly and genuinely servants of science and humanity. One possible approach to such self-knowledge is to retrace, more skeptically and critically, the steps through which we have individually acquired or own images of disabled people. In order to reject stereotypes in favor of more individualized, accurate perceptions, we must first recognize our own conditioned responses. Unrecognized stereotyping is itself a seriously handicapping condition.

WORKS CITED

For characters whose works are not cited, see: *The Oxford Classical Dictionary, The Oxford Companion to English Literature,* and *The Reader's Encyclopedia.*

Barnes, Ellen. "Developing Receptivity Toward Labelled Children," in Proceedings of the Special Study Institute, *Fostering Positive Attitudes Toward the Handicapped in School Settings,* May 1975, New York State Network of Special Education Instructional Materials Centers, State Education Department, Albany, New York.

Barrie, J.M. *Peter Pan*. New York: Scribner's, 1904.

Betjeman, John. "Portrait of a Deaf Man," *Collected Poems*. London: J. Murray, 1970.

Crane, Steven. "The Monster," *The Monster and Other Stories*. Harper, 1901.

Dickens, Charles. *Pickwick Papers*. 1837; rpt. Bridgeport, CT: Airmont, 1968.

Dostoevski, Feodor. *The Brothers Karamazov*. 1880; rpt. New York: Norton, 1976.

Dostoevski, Feodor. *The Idiot*. 1868; rpt. New York: Dell, 1961.

Duerrenmatt, Freidrich. *The Visit*. 1956; rpt. New York: Grove, 1962.

Gallico, Paul. *Snow Goose*. New York: Alfred Knopf, 1941.

Goldman, James. *The Lion in Winter*. New York: Random House, 1966.

Haley, Alex. *Roots*. Garden City, NY: Doubleday, 1976.

Heyward, DuBose. *Porgy*. 1925. Basis of the opera by George Gershwin, *Porgy and Bess*. 1935.

Hugo, Victor. *The Hunchback of Notre Dame*. 1831; rpt. New York: Dutton, 1953.

Kesey, Ken. *One Flew Over the Cuckoo's Nest*. New York: Penguin, 1976.

Kubrick, Stanley, dir. *Dr. Strangelove or: How I Learned to Stop Worrying and Love the Bomb*. With Peter Sellers and George C. Scott. Columbia Pictures, 1964.

Lardner, Ring. *"Haircut" & Other Short Stories*. New York: Charles Scribners & Sons.

Lawrence, David H. *Lady Chatterly's Lover*. New York: Grove, 1969.

Lee, Harper. *To Kill a Mockingbird*. New York: Popular Library, 1977.

Leroux, Gaston, *The Phantom of the Opera*. Cutchogue, NY: Buccaneer Books, 1975.

Maugham, Somerset. *Of Human Bondage.* 1919; rpt. New York: Penguin, 1970.

McCullers, Carson. *The Heart Is a Lonely Hunter.* New York: Bantam, 1970.

Melville, Herman. *Moby Dick.* 1851; rpt. New York: Abrams, 1976.

Menotti, Gian-Carlo. *Amahl & the Night Visitors.* New York: McGraw-Hill, 1952.

McMurtry, Larry. *The Last Picture Show.* New York: Dell, 1974.

Owen, Wilfred. *The Poems of Wilfred Owen.* Ed. E. Blunden. New York: Viking Press, 1931.

Porter, Katherine Anne. *Ship of Fools.* New York: New American Library, 1972.

Shakespeare, William. "King Richard III." *The Complete Works of Shakespeare.* London: Oxford University Press, 1943.

Sheed, Wilfred. *People Will Always Be Kind.* New York: Dell, 1974.

Shelley, Mary W. *Frankenstein.* 1818; rpt. New York: Macmillan, 1961.

Steinbeck, John. *Of Mice and Men.* 1951; rpt. New York: Bantam, 1970.

Stevenson, Robert L. *Treasure Island.* 1883; rpt. New York: Macmillan, 1963.

Tey, Josephine. *Daughter of Time.* New York: Berkeley Publishing Corp., 1975.

Twain, Mark. *The Adventures of Huckleberry Finn.* New York: Penguin, 1978.

Wallace, Lew. *Ben-Hur.* New York: McKay, 1977.

Warren, Robert Penn. *All the King's Men.* 1946; rpt. New York: Bantam, 1973.

Williams, Tennesse. *The Glass Menagerie.* New York: New Directions, 1940.

COMING THROUGH: MANHOOD, DISEASE, AND THE AUTHENTIC SELF
by Leonard Kriegel

If the reality of any history is subject to the distortions of need, then the reality of one's own past is thrust against the dream of independent selfhood, of true authenticity, a process that stains one's coming-of-age rites here in America. To look at one's own past life is rather like staring at a slide through a microscope in a high school biology class: no matter what textbook and teacher may claim, a sense of sullen wonder emerges from the sight of that which, one suspects, was not really meant to be seen at all. And in the skeptical corners of the mind where one harbors such resistance, the evidence is not believed. Fluid curlicues and amorphous shapes are not the essence of reality but rather that into which textbook, teacher, and microscope have somehow conspired to transpose reality. As witness, the eye lacks certainty. The mind insists that something is missing—an element in which shape defines shape. Or self declares self. It is this missing something that one draws upon for an extended reality, a truth at the heart of the lesser truth the eye inaccurately perceives. In the self's resistance lies its authenticity.

It is to this resisting self that one must address himself when he speaks about the situation of the cripple in America, particularly now, when the cripple's situation can be viewed as a paradigm for the general situation of men in America. Simply to think about being an American man is to be drawn back into one's confrontations with the demands this America established long before any of us thrust his individual presence, his "I," into its midst. Who among us can afford the world's indifference? Each of us, cripple and normal alike, must define those states of siege in the midst of which he chooses to live. And each of us is bound to an isolation that remains a denial of the human solidarity for which we yearn. John Donne's well-known "No manne is an islande" has been quoted approvingly by philosophers and clergymen and teachers of literature for more than three hundred years. But the truth is that each of us is at least sometimes an island, if for no other reason than that the creation of a self to which we can offer a hard emotional allegiance is a remarkably lonely process. In the long run, there is no one, nothing, to depend upon other than that island of a self—cragged, rock-rimmed, pushing desperately out of the sea, and alone. Above all, alone.

In the mind, the heroic man springs to life, formed by the very accidents that have made him what he is. And formed, too, by the expectant passion with which the self early on learns to view what it can potentially become. In this, the task of the cripple is to face what the normal may choose to ignore. The normal has that option—at least temporarily. But the cripple is isolated. Despite the professional ministrations of those who are concerned with his welfare, who reach out to his plight, his *condition* is more intense, more critical, than they can afford to admit. Whatever else the world may label it, he defines his isolation as total. He cannot seize hold of those supports which give balance to the normal. He is both pariah and victim, to be pitied, shunned, pinned, labelled, categorized, classified, and sooner or later packed in the spiritual ice box of a sanitized society in the hope that he can be dealt with "humanely" in some even more sanitized society of the future. Other than the right *to be,* he can be permitted everything. *For* without the right to be, he is permitted nothing. His selfhood must be denied by the normal, since to admit that selfhood would be to include nature itself in the category of villain. Simply in order to survive, the cripple breaks the harmony of man with nature. My own braces and crutches, the spastic presence of a young woman with cerebral palsy, a middle-aged man's blind questioning of corridors and curbstones as he makes his way forward into an emptiness matched by the emptiness from which he stems—all are guaranteed to make the normal uncomfortable. One could easily add to the list of disease and injury. But to do so would be rather pointless. For what cripples share is not so much a phsyical condition—their differences are far more pronounced than differences between white and Black, gentile and Jew, Italian and Eskimo—as it is the experience of having been categorized by the normals. The cripple inflicts a collective presence on the world at the expense of his individuality.

One can see this in the literature that deals with cripples. It is the nature of the thing viewed that is held up for the world's examination. An yet, in the most brutal as well as in the most generous portrayals of the crippled person in literature, there is something usually withheld, a dimension to his existence which indicates that even the greatest of writers are reluctant to come to terms with this particular being. In Melville's *The Confidence Man,* the cripple is a mere variation on a masquerade. Not even Captain Ahab in *Moby Dick* gets beyond his creator's demonology. The cripple in literature can be shadowed forth in the pious sentimentality of Dicken's Tiny Tim in *A Christmas Carol* or more fully fleshed out in the malign thrust for power which motivates Shakespeare's Richard the Third, but there is invariably something held back, an agonizing thruth in which the cripple assumes the role of brother under the bone. To recognize that would be to recognize his true fragility, the "humanness" which he shares with the normal. The cripple's dream is to force the rest of the world to recognize his wound as wound and not as mere category. It is the threat of visibility which ultimately accounts for his dismissal. Tiny Tim, for example, is not so much the creation of Dickens the artist as he is the literary embodiment of those social pressures which force the cripple to disguise his actual self, his *real* self, beneath the platitudes of Christian pieties which simply bury the very possibility of Tiny Tim's emerging as an individual character. Tiny Tim cannot be permitted to be, to act for himself; instead, he is acted upon, and even when he helps "change" Scrooge for the better he knows that it is a change in which Scrooge's newly purchased goodness will overwhelm his own. If he has learned nothing else, Tiny Tim has long since learned who can give and who must take. He has grown up with the experience of his own crippledness in a household in which he is more or less considered special, both a gift from God and a responsibility for man. Were the portrait truthful, he would be terrified to carry so heavy a burden on his weak back. But Dickens knew his audience. His Tiny Tim is content enough to serve as inspiration for others. The only thing he will carry on his back is the world's illusions.

Both Ahab and Richard the Third are more complex. But Ahab is so powerful a creation that he tends to overwhelm his readers. It is sometimes difficult to remember his wooden leg, for his symbolic presence rivals that of his adversary, Moby-Dick. If he is man, he is man removed from the world of nature not by his wound but by his will. Richard emerges from his crippledness in a different way. He is more human, certainly more recognizeable to anyone who is himself a cripple. Because we can see ouselves in him, he inspires a certain admiration. His desire is for vengeance. If what the world has done to him has been spawned by the indifference of accident, *his condition* remains a constant reminder of his need for vengeance—and vengeance visibly expressed and actively sought. His power and determination provoke admiration even from those for whom the cripple is threat. It is his recognition of his needs along with his insistence on defining himself for himself that sets him so singularly apart from Tiny Tim. And his relationship to the universe is that of a single individual, a man alone, rather than, as we suspect with Ahab, that of principle against principle. Richard *imposes* his broken body on the world; he forces life to accept him—even if it can accept him only as villain, the physical embodiment of spiritual evil. But what proves so attractive in his portrayal is that Richard decides that the world must accept the self he declares as his own, a self he has cunningly and laboriously and courageously earned. He must be what he is, so that if the world chooses to acknowledge his evil it must first acknowledge the essential fact of his personal presence. And he has, as few cripples do, the pleasure of demanding an accounting for his life, even if that accounting leads to his death. That he is among Shakespeare's great villains is a tribute to the depth of perception that went into his character. His effect on the cripple is a heightening of defiance, the subversive idea that, like Richard, he must struggle first to claim a self in order to understand what the world knows as *his condition.*

There are other examples in literature which provide a sense of a singular wound made powerful and attractive. D. H. Lawrence's remarkable story, "The Blind Man," is particularly notable since it comes from a writer who created what is still perhaps the cruelest caricature of the cripple that we have in all of English or American literature, the impotent Clifford Chatterly of *Lady Chatterly's Lover*. But no literature can be anything other than a reflection of those images of pain the world itself fears. It is not literature, whether good or bad, that will change those images. If men cannot entirely refashion their worlds, they can certainly exert a collective pressure towards change, a gathering of momentum. And this is the task of neither Lawrence nor Shakespeare nor any future Lawrence or Shakespeare. It is, rather, a question of how the cripple himself can turn his attention to the possibilities provided by his search for the personal self, the authentic man. And it is to the primacy of *his* performance, in the face of decisive, frequently overwhelming, odds to which he must address himself. He must discover in his own life, in what the outside world still calls *his condition*, a model for survival and heroism. Not only must he force an unwilling world to acknowledge his presence, he must also rediscover an essential aspect of the quest for manhood in America, the fact that accident is a form of opportunity. "A piece of the body torn out by the roots might be more to the point," wrote the young James Agee as he tried to explain why he had thrust the lives of Southern sharecroppers before his readers in 1940. For the cripple, the line embodies his own life—and it tells him that if survival is not reward enough it remains a source of pride. To have "come through" is every man's dream; for the cripple, it is a definition of the individual self's integrity.

How can the cripple handle his own burgeoning selfhood and yet deny what must inevitably come to be the primary fact of that selfhood, his functioning as a cripple? If his quest is for an authentic self that he can view as his alone, how, then, can he avoid turning his visible stigma into an invisible source of strength, an asset designed to claim not only the world's attention but also—and sooner or later he is going to have to admit this, too—it's admiration? The answer to such questions can provide the cripple with a way out of the dilemmas created by categorization by others. It is here that he is offered the opportunity to define himself for himself, only he must take the risk of holding up the true ragged ends of his existence. And for all to see. It is exactly here that he can point the way for others, the normals of the world, as they confront the demanding self in a time of mendacious conformity, a time in which the very concept of an authentic self has been virtually buried beneath dull variations on doing one's "own thing."

That the odds are formidable is obvious. The control of one's destiny, even having a voice in one's destiny, is at best problematical for anyone; for the cripple, such control is bound to be even more problemmatical. Chance is an even greater element in his life than it is in the lives of others. Having already witnessed the power of accident, he knows that if the reconciliation of the individual self's wishes with the world's actualities can lead to what we call maturity it can also lead to madness and despair and suicide. The terror of performance resides in the heart's desire to measure up to what one believes to be the demands normals meet on an everyday life. Perhaps the world's charge can be diminished, but it can never be wholly ignored, never forgotton. The image of what one *was crashes against the fantasy of what one might have been. Under the best of circumstances, maturity is temporary.*

The cripple's paradox is that the ultimate source of his individual potential is his wound, the only thing he possesses that is his and his alone. Curiously enough, so many of the primary texts of our time illuminate that potential and call upon us to acknowledge that the cripple fulfills the requirements of the contemporary. But I should like to focus upon only two of these texts, because each of them has had a certain influence on my own life and because each of them is concerned with the possibilities of the heroic in our time. What Norman Mailer's *The White Negro* and Ernest Becker's *The Denial of Death* share is a concern with the problems facing the individual self in a world in which individualism has become a synonym for conformity, a concern with what once was called "manhood." It is not a new concern, but it is one for which, quite suddenly, the shared experience of the past seems inadequate. Men are trapped in a world not of their own choosing but decisively of their own making.

The cripple, on the other hand, is trapped not so much by his condition as by his failure to recognize the true imperatives of that condition. He has actually been handed a map of possibilities. Only he still must learn to read maps. In speaking about Kierkegaard as a psychoanalyst, Becker notes how defiance illuminates authenticity:

> And this brings us to our final type of man: the one who asserts himself out of defiance of his own weakness, who tries to be a god unto himself, the master of his fate, a self-created man. He will not be merely the pawn of others, of society; he will not be a passive sufferer and secret dreamer, nursing his own inner flame in oblivion. He will plunge into life.

A highly dramatic, almost volatile, passage, a call to life that would have been better understood in the Nineteenth Century, a demand that one embrace what Becker so cogently labels "defiant self-creation" in the pursuit of existence, even if it must manifest itself as "a revolt against existence itself." Of course, Becker did not have the cripple in mind at all. But merely to point this out and leave it is to retreat into being an object to be classified by others. Men work out of the terrors of their own immediacies. Becker himself was to die shortly after the publication of *The Denial of Death*, and it remains a book that one cannot read without suspecting that its author approached its composition with his own impending death on the brittle edges of consciousness. And this despite his death-bed denial (one is tempted to suggest that the death-bed denial is a kind of proof of the thing itself). How else can one account for the particular clarity his sentences possess for the cripple? How else can one read a passage such as the following?

In a word, illness is an object. We transfer to our own body as if it
were a friend on whom we can lean for strength or an enemy who
threatens us with danger. At least it makes us feel real and gives us
a little purchase on our fate.

For Becker, man can be neither resigned nor accepting. That he sees the terrible need modern man has for a heroic potential is obvious. But as an anthropologist, he understands, too, that the heroic emerges out of man's view of
himself in the modern world. It is this king of perspective, an anthropological
perspective, if you will, that leads him to speak of the very concept of mental
illness as being no more than "a way of talking about people who have lost
courage, which is the same as saying that it reflects the failure of heroism."
Mailer is different; he is more grudgingly Western, more American. *The White
Negro* is as seminal in its impatience as it is in its message. Mailer is no lover of
mankind, and his prose is steeped in an anger that borders on apocolyptic rage.
For Mailer, the crime of modern man, the crime of the much-berated
bourgeoisie, is not so much the failure of courage as it is the prevention of
courage in others. Mailer sees manhood itself as having been betrayed, and it is
this, as much as anything else, which accounts for the sense of brooding
violence which erupts in each of his books like a dust-storm in New Mexico,
quick and violent and blocking out anything else in the landscape. The
political fear that he discovers in Eisenhower's America itself evolves into a
metaphor for timidity of purpose. Men long for direction, are made quiscent by
technology. (It is characteristic of the vagueness of Mailer's thought and the
kind of shotgun effect of his rhetoric that he seems to conceive of technology as
being both totalitarian and feminine.)

A stench of fear has come out of every pore of American life, and
we suffer from a collective failure of nerve. The only courage, with
rare exceptions, that we have been witness to, has been the isolated
courage of isolated people.

In the Fifties, at least Mailer desperately wanted to force men out of their times.
Ultimately the only herosim he was able to postulate in *The White Negro* is
that of those who consciously defy the meretricious in themselves by struggling
against a society that is both timid and conventional. One cannot blame Mailer
for the explosion of self-conscious unconventionality we witnessed in the late
Sixties and early Seventies. Writing in 1955, Mailer probably had no way of
knowing that his ushering forth the hipster who models his life on that of the
Negro was to find an audience so bored with its perogatives and so distant from
the ideas which had fed its parents that it would simply emerge as one more
American variation on what Harold Rosenberg once called New York intellec-
tuals, "that herd of independent minds." The self on exhibition is yet the self
denied.

As writing, *The White Negro* is not one of Mailer's more memorable perfor-
mances. The prose is often rhetorical and mushy, as Mailer gives way to a lack of
artistic structure in his effort to forge an outlaw vision of the individual's relationship to society. And yet, as is so frequently Mailer's saving grace, it is a pro-

se that lives with its own incapacities, its own plunging romanticism. One is tempted to say that Mailer turns the very vagaries of his argument into a kind of intimate defiance of conventional American society. In his adulation of the hipster, it is not violence as violence that he praises but the need to find any imperative which will affirm the self's capacity to endure, which will enable post-War American man to move toward a belief in his ability both to accept tests and to deny the legitimacy of those who insist on testing him. Behind the convoluted prose is an idea which has grown in importance since 1955—that a technological society makes it almost impossible to be either a man or a failure as a man because it so severely limits the areas in which any individual can be legitimately challenged. "To be an existentialist," Mailer writes, "one must be able to feel oneself—one must know one's desires, one's rages, one's anguish, one must be aware of the character of one's frustration and know what would satisfy it."

In so singular a manner is the white hipster transformed into the black outlaw. But is there any contemporary figure to whom these words are more applicable than they are to the cripple? For to be a cripple is to recognize how fragile, how vulnerable, the self actually is, how easily the needs of the ego, the demands that spring out of one's desire to take vengeance upon a world indifferent to one's fate, can be twisted away from their potential fulfillment, broken off, left to lie with the debris that line one's mind like driftwood washed up on shore after a hurricane. The necessity of action is a consistent reminder of the limitations of the body. In the mind, those limitations can still be exceeded. In real life, in the actual here and now, one is tied to a particular lack, a disability, an invisible enemy which has left visible damage upon one's own body. There is no enemy with which one can live on terms of greater intimacy. So pressing a realization leads, at first, to a rage so massive as to seem insurmountable. Nor does it offer the cripple solace to point out, with Becker, that disease can be looked at as "an *object*, an adversary, something against which to marshall one's courage; disease and dying are still *living* processes in which one is engaged." Rage remains the legacy, the terribly visible sign of stimatization, even more than the condition that gave birth to that rage.

But matched against that rage are the possibilities of selfhood. It is exactly here that the cripple can thrust himself forward, can offer himself as an alternative to technological castration, and can invoke the authority of his very existence as a legitimate way of using masculinity. He can display his capacity to measure himself against his fate, to exist with the harsh growl of endurance in his mouth, to create psychic capital out of his ability to live under duress. At this point in our history, the cripple is the best example we have of how endurance can be transcribed into defiance. And it is because of his endurance that the cripple discovers that he can define the possibilities of the heroic in himself; it is here that he senses he has pulled even with the normals of this world, has managed to shape the paradoxes and dilemmas of his existance into an attitude with which he can confront the world. After all, if one seeks models of the existential hero in the Negro or the rebellious young, then how much more truthful would it not be to seek those models in lives which have been forced to barter a part of their substance, a part of their very grounding on this earth, simply in order to survive. Whether we admit it or not, the reality lies there before us, literally at our feet. The language of contemporary resistance can still be voiced only by that now-unfashionable philosophy of existentialism. For it remains the only philosophy we have which still insists on the self's right *to be* in the face of a universe that is at best indifferent and at worst actively hostile. It is the living sound of our everyday lives. Here is Mailer defining his heroic model:

> If the fate of twentieth-century man is to live with death from adolescence to premature senescence, why then the only live-giving answer is to accept the terms of death, to live with death as immediate danger, to divorce oneself from society, to exist without roots, to set out on that uncharted journey into the rebellious imperatives of the self.

Of course, this was written in the mid-Fifties. But it embodies a point-of-view which I suspect is even more applicable to our time, for if the two decades that followed taught us nothing else, they taught us to be afraid of that which exists outside of our individual confines. I do not mean to suggest that one seek to engulf his being in the heaviness of Mailer's prose, nor even in the apocolyptic nature of its vision, a vision which Mailer himself finally speaks of, in language that should embarrass all of us, as "the decision to encourage the psychopath in oneself." Whatever else American life lacks, it has more than its fair share of psychopaths, most of them battling to inflict their presence on us during the seven o'clock television news. But what Mailer captures in this essay is the necessity to defy one's fate, to carve a being from the very indifference with which the world-at-large views one. And no one I know of lives on more intimate terms with this than does the cripple. It is simply impossible to have come through as a cripple, to have claimed a self, without understanding the innumerable times one places one's life in an unusual intimacy with death. One quite literally and unrhetorically lives with "death as immediate danger." That which the normals take for granted is for the cripple an explosion of possibilities, many of them demanding of him a courage that is disproportionate to anything normals have to muster. To write this is embarrassing; it is also true. The terms on which I live my everyday life are essentially inconceiveable to my normal friends. The crippled self's need to define the absolute limits of its being through the limits of what it shall attempt—and to do this both clearly and consciously—makes even the everyday quite extraordinary.

I am still haunted by a memory that seems to me a paradigm of the existential nature of the way in which the cripple faces the demands of the self he has brought into being. As a senior in college, I happened to go to a party in an old, dimly-lit tenement in what today is known as the East Village but at that time was still known as the Lower East Side. The apartment turned out to be up four rather steep flights of stairs in a building that looked as if it had simply lingered from a 1930s Dead End kids movie. The staircase was broken into three separate landings for each flight, which created an empty space of about four feet running down the heart of the staircase from the roof on the fifth floor to the bottom entrance. I remember feeling that I was staring down an unused mine shaft as I made my way up the stairs. The dim light provided by twenty-five watt bulbs at the head of each landing made the illusion even stronger. But going up the stairs proved be no problem. Some four hours later, filled with good conversation and food and wine, I began my descent. Since the only bannister was on the left hand side as I went up, I was forced to descend the stairs backwards. All during the party, which I remember having thoroughly enjoyed, I had been thinking of that descent. I had considered asking someone to accompany me downstairs, but I dismissed that thought as a form of humiliation. Capacity is measured by the self. I had brought no one to the party. And I would depart alone.

In order to descend the stairs, I had to hold one of my crutches with my left thumb, jam it tightly against the bannister, put my weight on my right crutch, and maneuver my legs into the semi-darkness behind me until I felt the next step beneath my feet. At the head of each landing, in order to gain the leverage I needed to descend, I would do a fireman's lift and drape my body across the bannister, so that from the waist up I found myself leaning into empty space, my weight fused on that left hand which grasped both bannister and crutch. The only thing that kept me from falling through space to crash to the tiled floor some forty or so feet below me was the strength in my left arm.

I cannot remember a moment when life seemed to me more immediate, more tensile with its own promise, than it did as I leaned across that landing into hostile space. It was as if the accident of having lost my legs to polio at the age of eleven had finally been met head on. To be conscious that the only thing keeping me from crashing to my death below was the power in *my* arms and the insistence that I could now, if only in this seemingly minor action, determine the course of my fate, filled me with what I can only describe as a surge of joy. Like Wordsworth, I was "surprised by joy"—but the surprise emanted from the inner self, not from nature. I remember a distinct voice that seemed to cry out from the very chambers of my heart, "You are a cripple! And to be a cripple is to be different." The need to prove the self's capacity, its legitimate toughness, held me suspended four stories above that dingy tiled entrance of a Lower East Side tenement.

Such memories are today embarrassing, particularly to a forty-four year old college professor who likes to believe that he is as sardonically rational as any of his colleagues. And yet, the particular memory must be served. Since the age of eleven, I had lived "with death as immediate danger," and I would live that way for the rest of my life. To pretend otherwise would be to lie. And to universalize my fate would be a different lie. Suspended in space, it was as if I had to encompass the myths of my own existence, to accept as meaningful in myself the peculiar pleasures of combat that mark the life of the cripple. The experience was to be repeated again and again in my life, but always to fuse with that moment of realization when I hung above the tiled entrance, hung above my future. If it was never again to provide quite the same sense of exhilaration, it was to remain a vivid reminder of how one might go about attacking life. For the cripple, knowledge of how he has been wounded by accident is exceeded only by the knowledge of how intimate the future terms of his existence must be. The path to the authentic self is through the acceptance of the risks of disease, the legacy of accident.

This is not to say that the cripple merely invokes an inverted Cartesianism: "I suffered; therefore, I am." To accept this would be to accept the passivity that has traditionally been the cripple's fate. What he must accept, rather, is the *stigmatization* of his wound; he must learn to look upon himself as a man engaged in the creation of a suitable destiny. It is a need voiced by existential psychology, a need which demands an almost religious conception of the individual self. Perhaps it even demands a movement back towards the territory occupied by Tiny Tim. But with this substantive difference—the recognition that if one is hovering above the tiled floor, then the enmity of nature becomes the very blood of life for the self. To have suffered the experience of permanent disability is a path to intimacy with God only as it negates the idea of suffering as a good. Suffering is meant to be remembered, but not to dominate, not to transform one into an object—even an object of sanctification—for others. It is by now axiomatic to write that it is better to resist fate than to resign oneself to it, better to condemn false piety in order to ask necessary questions, better to recognize that the cost of becoming what the French termed "man engaged" is a cost that chips away at the individual self. No, not suffering, but the knowledge of having come through, is the source of one's pride. One approaches such pride cautiously, inch by inch, as he tries to frame those moments which have proven to be decisive in the self's quest. Given the inevitable swell of challenge and response as they exist in the mind, that past is transformed, from harbinger to beacon, from death to life. The admission is made: "This is the man I dreamed of being. But here is the man I am yet going to be." To seize one's fate is to take back the past.

This is not to advocate that the cripple assume that his stigma, his wound, is now to be the glory of *his condition*. It is, rather, resistance to the rush of circumstance, the denial of the inevitability of accident, that sets him apart. Adversity is to be faced honestly, on the level of its own presentation. What the cripple must do is to match the potential for response to any situation with the peculiar manner in which that situation breaks against him *because* he is a cripple. The measure of manhood can become the capacity of one's rage. And it is this, I believe, that we mean when we speak of "endurance." There is no proper approach to one's own limitations or one's potential failures. There is a quality of risk to any experience and it is this that we learn to cherish. To endow the normal world with a kind of purposeful malignity is to make it more difficult to understand than it is. One of the reasons why a writer like Mailer continues to seem so essential is that he is able to recognize the extent to which rage can be an endowment. Blind as his anger may sometimes seem, it is far more useful than resignation—and far more capable of making sense out of the modern, too. Defiance is superior to resignation, because, and the word itself has become almost an embarrassment, it is simply more "manly."

Of course, the answer to contemporary masculine confusion here in America is not to be found in a quick dose of cerebral palsy or the experience of a congenital disease. But to live with a decisive physical impairment, and *to live consciously* with that impairment, letting it chart one's existence like a beacon on a stormy night at sea, to do this is to accept both the possibility and the risks of the emergence of a true self, an Individual "I," forged by the specific attributes which accident has given it. To defy one's destiny is a statement of purpose, even if of negative purpose; it voices one's refusal to accept the irremediable as long as there are alternatives to be glimpsed. The failure to recognize the human significance of this is where Lawrence, in both "The Blind Man" and *Lady Chatterly's Lover,* went wrong; it is where Dickens and Melville went wrong, too. Only Shakespeare, who possessed a receptive eye for the truly demonic, captured it in his Richard the Third—and even there it lies partly hidden beneath the political machinations we are asked to focus on. Richard's rage is compelling today because it remains a personal response to accident. The rage, as well as the man, insists that accident can be overcome. In the cripple, isolation must be made into a time of opportunity. Perhaps his fate, and that of the Negro, too, is to seize upon Emersonian individualism at the very moment in our history when it has proven itself bankrupt. Still, it is not an insignificant fate. If he must be categorized by those others, then let him, at least, earn the satisfaction of a self created out of his personal encounter with his agony. In this resides his manhood.

"Man is nothing but what he makes of himself," writes Sartre as he offers us a primer of existentialism. What continues to be appealing about existentialism, what may even paradoxically enough, explain its recent demise as a force among philosophers, is that its logic bequeaths itself to us as the legacy of our times. It is the mirror of what the world makes of us. Even before that incident of coming down the stairs which I have described, I can remember searching for a way in which I might turn my incapacity into my identity, a way in which I might force myself through the dead ends and dull surrenders that the world considered my due to pull an identity out of the reality I was forced to live with. The prospect which most frightened me was the prospect of being classified, of being, like Prufrock, left "pinned and wriggling on the wall." Everything I did could be challenged by others. In retrospect, the challenges were minor. What gave them life was that I myself had more or less been expected to believe them. My ego was receptive to the doubts of others, and the doubts of others could easily be transformed into my own. The process seemed endless. No matter what I did, no matter how well I thought I performed (and it is much too simple to belittle the concept of performance as something endemic only to American men), what inevitably haunted me was what could so easily be seized upon by the normals, those others. Performance remained the measure of success to the extent that it was something that I had seized from my life, rather than something that had been given to me. Of course, one can protest that such lack of surety is endemic to all men and to all women, cripple and normal alike. No one can ever be certain that what is possessed has been taken from life rather than bestowed as a gift.

And yet, on the face of it, the cripple's situation obviously makes him more vulnerable to such doubts. He must first make his presence felt to himself; he must find a way to endorse selfhood by intimately acknowledging that it is his wound which has made him different. And he must accept the consequences of his actions, accept them totally and even gratefully, despite the fact that this may mean cutting himself off from others. I suspect that is for this reason that there are so few books about disease which can be termed truthful; the intent is so frequently to deny that which must be affirmed. The cripple must learn to look upon what had been stigmatization as an acquisition, to admit to having been set apart. The process was captured by the poet, Karl Shapiro, in "The Leg," a poem about an amputation suffered by a soldier during World War II. The soldier struggles to accept the loss of part of his body. He must learn to adapt to life without the leg, even as the life that he possesses extends his defiance of accident to the principle upon which his future is to be founded.

> Later, as if deliberately, his fingers
> Begin to explore the stump. He learns a shape
> That is comfortable and tucked in like a sock.
> This has a sense of humor, this can despise
> The finest surgical limb, the dignity of limping,
> The nonsense of wheelchairs. Now he smiles
>   to the wall:
> The amputation becomes an acquisition.

To make of injury acquisition, to make of disease a living symbol, and to do this not as an expression of resignation but of defiance—it is this which Shapiro's soldier achieves. His life will be different from that point on, for he has been tested and discovered not wanting. He has learned that he has come through, and along with the achievement of coming through, the pride in performance against great obstacles. Ultimately, he will learn to recognize the opportunity that fate has offered him, learn to trust his own disease, to trust the body which, in having betrayed his hopes and aspirations, had made a statement about his relationship to it and to the universe.

However difficult it may be to write such things today, the authentic self must still be won. And it is exactly here that the cripple comes to terms with what he is, here that he sees in the ironies and obligations of his experience our time's representative man. He has learned to accept the humiliation of pain by accepting, too, the fact that humiliation must be resisted even as it triumphs. To make light of the accident that creates his selfhood is to deny the true depths of the wound he experiences, to deprive it of significance because it is not something that the rest of the world can live with comfortably. But he does not have to do this in order to survive, even if it is what the world finds preferable. There are, after all, two kinds of endurance, and for his own sanity he must learn to distinguish between them: endurance as a quality that the outside world, the normals, insist on for his life; and endurance as the ability to define his own capacity, to retreat into the limitations of disease in order to accept, and to accept fully, even gratefully, the necessity of hurling mind and body against the restrictions that have been placed in his path. The idea of the self created by the self is a Nineteenth-Century concept, one that has perhaps never before in history been as unfashionable in America as it is at the present moment. But there is little else upon which the individual who demands authenticity can rely.

And yet, even the demanding self must recognize that defeat is implicit. Like death, disease is the reigning-in of mortality. The cripple's condition is the human condition, even if the vanity of coming through may at times feed his illusions. There is a point at which the acceptance of one's own wound, the living with the internal enemy who, as Becker writes, "threatens danger," leads to a certain haughtiness, perhaps even a certain contempt for those others, the normals, who have never been called upon to prove their capacity. If, as Sarte claims, man is "nothing else but what he makes of himself," than an unvoiced corollary of that statement is that the man who succeeds in creating an authentic self against great odds runs the risk of what used to be called the sin of pride. Everything he does, every act of love or hate, every victory he claims or defeat he suffers—each has been pulled from the fire. And the true "dirty little secret" of the cripple's world is the extent to which he takes pride in his performance and acknowledges his ability to force his presence upon the world. When one matches himself against his fate, it is almost inevitable that the normal's frame of reference comes to seem comic, even, at time, ludicrous. Picture, if you will, a man or woman who lives on intimate terms with pain as a condition of his daily existence listening to the stentorian nasality of Howard Cosell praising the "courage" of an athlete who earns his $250,000 a year salary on aching knees.

At this point, the cripple must recognize that the normal person can absorb his reality. A man may choose to create an authentic self out of his defiance of circumstance, but he cannot re-make the nature of existence. No matter what the will demands, dead legs do not run nor do sightless eyes see. The knowledge of what we are cannot be avoided for long. Memory pinches one's heroism. And there is never a second chance to set things right, to make your destiny an extenion of your vision. Years ago, I wrote an autobiography in which I tried to re-create with neither sentimentality nor false piety the experience of having had polio. When I first sat down to write *The Long Walk Home,* I assumed that what would prove to be difficult would be those scenes in which I re-lived the pain, the sense of helplessness, the loss of dignity that the onset of disease inevitably produces. To my surprise, these scenes proved easy to handle; they virtually wrote themselves. What actually proved difficult to write about truthfully were all those minor wars which ended in no-so-minor defeats—falling at a subway exit and waiting for someone to pick me up, daydreaming about the strength and power I knew were rightfully mine only to look in the mirror and find reality mocking my very presence.

I suppose that I would still call *The Long Walk Home* an honest book, but I can also now see how decisively it speaks of my own limitations of vision. "At the cost of legs, I had won a self. How much cheaper a price could I have expected to pay?" With these two sentences the book ends. And in a lifetime during which I have written my fair share of sentences better forgotten, I can think of no sentence as singularly untruthful as that last. I would give a great deal to be able to take it back today. For I know now how truly expensive such victories are, how fragmentary, how terribly short-lived, how ludicrous to call the price "cheap," and how essentially demeaning to the legitimate and painful demands I had made upon myself.

But fate has a way of pinching us all with reminders. A few months after my book was published, I found myself in a small Dutch fishing village. I was feeling smug about that self I had fashioned, like a man who draws for a five card straight in poker and discovers that he has pulled a royal flush instead. I was in the Netherlands on a Fulbright; the book, my first, had been published to rather favorable reviews; and I had just received both tenure and a promotion at the New York college at which I still teach. One sunny October day, I was walking with my two year old son on the concrete embankment that paralleled the beach. My son waddled on down the embankment, waving for me to follow him. He walked about ten yards or so into the sand and then stopped to wait. And I did follow him, for I was suddenly filled with a sense of selfhood won that was so absolute that the illusion of power was even greater than what I had felt hovering above that tiled floor some nine years earlier. It was an illusion so vivid that it literally devoured the reality of experience. I was insanely certain that I could follow him onto that beach, pick him up on my shoulders, cast braces and crutches away, and run against the North Sea wind—a normal American father with his laughing American son. It was another token of existential absurdity, one that would have brought a smile to Kierkegaard's lips, if not to Sarte's. Man makes himself, but he never re-makes his circumstances—except, of course, in his fantasies. When my crutches hit the sand, they sank, which is what crutches usually do on beaches. Not only would I not run, I could not even walk after a two year old. And I found myself overwhelmed by a rage so pure, total, and all-devouring that it must have been that one step away from madness about which we speak so often. My mind was capable of such violence that I could have passed through that Dutch fishing village like a whirlwind of vengeance for the thwarted self. Instead, I retreated to the firmness of the concrete embankment to wait, angry and humiliated, for my two year old son to realize that his father could not follow him onto the beach. The price is never cheap. And that authentic self is never quite won. It recedes from the cripple's grasp, just as it can never really be won by the normal—except, of course, in one's fantasies, which create the language of their own fulfillment. There is, after all, the unlikely possibility that a two year old boy will possess the patience and understanding of Job. But even when the fantasies evaporate, there is the final lesson that the wound imposes. It, too, must be absorbed. Dignity as a man consists of the terms of the struggle we declare. And to live consciously means to live honstely, to speak of the authentic self as something which has been borrowed for the moment, borrowed for its own sake, and for the sake of all the sons waiting on the beach.

WORKS CITED

Becker, Ernest. *Denial of Death.* Riverside, NY: Free Press, 1973.

Dickens, Charles. *A Christmas Carol.* 1843; rpt. New York: Dutton, 1972.

Kriegel, Leonard. *The Long Walk Home.* New York: Appleton-Century, 1964.

Lawrence, David H. "The Blind Man." *Complete Short Stories.* New York: Penguin.

_____. *Lady Chatterly's Lover.* 1928; rpt. New York: Grove, 1969.

Mailer, Norman. *The White Negro.* Eugene, OR: City Lights, 1957.

Melville, Herman. *The Confidence Man.* 1857; rpt. New York: Norton, 1971.

Melville, Herman. *Moby Dick.* 1851; rpt. New York: Abrams, 1976.

Shakespeare, William. "King Richard III." *The Complete Works of Shakespeare.* London: Oxford Univ. Press, 1943.

Shapiro, Karl. "The Leg." *Collected Poems, 1940-1978.* New York: Random House, 1978.

THE FAMILY'S VIEW
OF THE FUTURE

by Seymour Sarason

When parents have a child their lives are forever changed and at the time of birth, the changes they foresee are almost always positive. They may be aware of but do not dwell on the complications and obligations that can introduce stress in their lives. Economic, psychological, sexual, physical, recreational — these are areas of functioning that may be adversely affected by having to care for a developing child. Even when a child is developing according to norms, the nature of the balance between satisfactions and dissatisfactions, between personal freedom and frustration, changes for all members of the family.

Several decades ago the balance in the relationship between positive and negative factors was clearly in the favor of the positive — witness the capacity of marriages to stay intact. Today, however, with the dramatic increase in the rate of divorce, marriage and the family have become more fragile institutions. In no way does this imply that the increase is due in large part to the stresses engendered by rearing children, but it does suggest that the attitudes and expectations people bring to marriage decrease their tolerance for frustration. And when we bear in mind that increasingly women as well as men will be planning a life-long working career, the problems surrounding child rearing can be expected to put added burdens on marital and family stability. All of this is by way of saying that fantasy and reality, great expectations and the restrictions of marriage and family, are polarities that few families seem to balance satisfactorily.

If what I have said characterizes the family with "normal" children, we would expect that the vulnerability of a family would become greater when it confronts that task of rearing a retarded child. But this expectation cannot be demonstrated by data, because the relevant studies have not been done. Grossman's study (1972) did indicate that many brothers and sisters seemed to have benefitted from having a retarded sibling, but she cautioned that the number of these instances would probably be far less on a percentage basis if she had chosen her subjects in a way more representative of the population of families with retarded children. Also, Grossman studied only normal siblings and it was from them that she obtained an indirect and admittedly incomplete picture of family life and dynamics. And as she emphasizes, social-economic factors played an important role; to this point we shall return later.

There is still another factor that should temper expectations: the development in the past two decades of community programs that never existed before and that have enabled families to cope better with their retarded children. One would expect, for example, that the description of the dispiriting and disabling consequences for families with retarded children reported by the Carvers (a study done in the fifties but published in 1972) would be inapplicable to the current scene. Although this may be true, experience suggests that it is less true than some people would like us to believe. There can be no doubt that the recent changes in society's verbal expressions about the needs and rights of retarded children and their families, accompanied as these have been by dramatic increases in public funds for a wide array of programs and services, have been helpful to families, especially when these families are compared to those only two decades ago. But as we shall see later, just as we should not uncritically accept the belief that the presence of a retarded child in a family has only catastrophic effects, we should not smugly assume that increased funding and programs have dramatically and positively altered the experience of families. The history of the field of mental retardation contains too many instances in which progress was confused with increased expenditures or public resolves to give more than lip service to the idea of humane treatment.

In 1843 Dorothea Dix gave her famous impassioned, searing address to the Massachusetts legislature detailing the inhumane conditions of the state's "humane" institutions. We like to believe that in the century following that address the conditions she described were eliminated, and that humaneness was restored to its appropriate governing role in this sphere of human affairs. But in 1967 Burton Blatt described similar conditions to the same legislature. There is a difference between change and progress!

SOMETHING HAPPENED

Something Happened is a novel by Joseph Heller published in 1974 to wide critical acclaim. The major themes of the book are by no means new: the driven, competitive, materialistic, married Don Juanish American male whose personal and familial instability and disintegration increase as he climbs the ladder of "success." The book is an indictment of many aspects of our society, and although it describes a tragedy, it does contain, as one would expect from the author of *Catch-22,* zany and comical moments. By the end of the story the narrator and central character, Slocum, is a prematurely aged, empty, lost soul bereft of any social intimacies or anchors. To those around him, Slocum appears whole, but he is really far down the road toward going to pieces. Inquiry into how this came about is beyond our purposes here. Suffice it to say that Heller, unlike most of us, gives no simple cause-and-effect explanation. Indeed, he gives not "causes" but rather shows us that the lives of people are too inextricably interwoven to permit applying the usual cause-and-effect type of explanation.

What is relevant to our purpose is that Slocum is the father of three children, one of whom is Derek, brain damaged and mentally retarded from birth. What picture is drawn about Derek's perceived effects on the family as a unit and on

66

each of its members as individuals? It is not surprising that the clearest picture we get is of Slocum. To say that he is ambivalent toward the child would be misleading because this would obscure that fact that his negative feelings are more frequent and stronger than his positive ones. He is, of course, guilt-ridden because of the way he feels but, nevertheless, he admits his dislike for the child, if only to himself. When Slocum reviews the birth of the child and the dry, insensitive way in which Derek's diagnosis was communicated; the maddening unhelpfulness of the physicians; his early attempts to interact with the child and the lack of the kind or responsiveness Derek could give in return; the kind and quality of person hired to take care of Derek; his own unwillingness to interact with families who also had retarded children; his wife's complete unwillingness to consider institutionalizing the child; the worry about what would happen to Derek if something happened to him and his wife — these ruminations exacerbate other keenly felt personal disappointments and inadequacies. Slocum would rather have Derek dead, not because Slocum is a hateful or sadistic person, but because the child is such an obvious reminder of almost all of the father's vulnerabilities. Derek was not a "cause" but an addition to a social-familial context, a web of interrelationships whose strands varied considerably in strength, durability, and historical origins.

We are given less detail about the reactions of Slocum's family to Derek. His wife's personal slide downhill, social withdrawal, and alcoholism are not attributed only to Derek, toward whom she seems to have a religious and protective but aloof attitude. The one thing we are told about Derek's two siblings is that the sister worries that Derek's presence in the family may interfere with her social attractiveness to men. The members of this family increasingly become strangers to each others, just as they see Derek as an object who is "there:" empty, unresponsive, unconnected.

And what about Derek himself? What kind of *person* is he? We are told next to nothing. It is as if no one inside or outside the family ever considered Derek as a human being deserving a different kind of thought and attention. From the moment Derek's condition was "diagnosed" the world seemed to give up on him. Since money was no problem, Derek received "care;" there was always hired help to be with him. He had custodians, but there is not the faintest suggestion that anyone was devoted to him as a human being with some capability, however modest, for development. And so the author leaves the reader with the impression that Derek was what he is because of his "condition," as if he does not inevitably reflect how he is perceived and treated. The self-fulfilling prophecy has claimed another victim.

Something Happened may be fiction, but it is faithful to what frequently occurs in reality in several important respects. First, the impact of the retarded child on the family has to be seen in the context of the existing strengths and weaknesses of the marital relationship. Second, the developmental fate of a retarded child has to be understood in light of the marital relationship. Third, no member of the family escapes the impact of the retarded individual, be that impact positive, negative, or (more likely) both. Fourth, the family tends to view proferred help has inadequate, ineffective, and even inappropriate. Fifth, there are forces in our society that engender and reinforce personal isolation and feelings of loneliness so that when a personal or family tragedy occurs, it tends to aggravate these feelings. When we talk about the retarded child we must never forget that that child is in a particular family in a particular society at a particular time. There are societies quite different from ours and it is not surprising therefore, that in some of them the family and social surroundings would perceive and react to Derek in a fashion quite opposite to that described in Heller's novel. To understand the significance of this point, the reader is urged to read Eaton and Weil's study of Hutterite society (1955).

AGING AND THE PASSAGE OF TIME

Near the end of the novel, immediately after Slocum makes another unsatisfying attempt to establish rapport with his favorite child, Derek's brother, he mourns to himself:

> My memory's failing, my bladder is weak, my arches are falling, my tonsils and adenoids are gone, and my jawbone is rotting, and now my little boy wants to cast me away and leave me behind for reasons he won't give me. What else will I have? My job? When I am fifty-five, I will have nothing more to look forward to than Arthur Baron's job and reaching sixty-five. When I am sixty-five, I will have nothing more to look forward to than reaching seventy-five, or dying before then. And when I am seventy-five, I will have nothing more to look forward to than dying before eighty-five, or geriatric care in a nursing home. I will have to take enemas. (Will I have to be dressed in double-layer waterproof undershorts designed especially for incontinent gentlemen?) I will be incontinent. I don't want to live longer than eighty-five, and I don't want to die sooner than a hundred and eighty-six.
>
> Oh, my father — why have you done this to me?
>
> I want him back.
>
> (pp. 523-524)

For Slocum the future, like the present, is oppressive and prolonged. Throughout the novel he fears that tomorrow will be like today, and next year like this one. He does not reach for the future. Instead, he longs for a past when he did not have to protect others, but when others protected him. It is as if he feels that his life is over and the future will be mere existence, a kind of penance for past misdeeds visited on him by fate. Slocum feels old, very old, and psychologically he is like an aged person who waits, sometimes eagerly, to meet death. It would be simplistic, as we have emphasized, to attribute Slocum's view of the future only to the consequences of Derek's retardation. Derek is but one strand, albeit an important one, in the fabric of Slocum's social living that suffuses the future with anxiety, loneliness, and pathetic dependence. Heller is describing well how a person's particular sense of the passage of time is one of the core ingredients of the sense of aging. The sense of aging is *not* a function of chronological age (Becker, 1973), but of events and experiences that make one feel that the best of life has passed and the future is a downhill slide. *This concern with the passage of time and a sense of a foreboding future, along with those obsessive thoughts about one's death and its consequences for one's kin, are almost never absent in parents of retarded children. Indeed, historically speaking, these parents as a group knew about the poignancy of the aging process long before it became a topic of public concern.* And this is what Heller's artistry has shown.

When Slocum was told about Derek's retardation, it was like a bomb was thrown into a smoldering volcano. Suddenly, his accustomed view of the future changed. It was no longer imagined as an endless upward and onward course, but more like a mine field in which he was trapped. He was hemmed in and that was the way it was always going to be. And what if he died? Where would Derek go? Who would take care of him? And when Slocum fantasized about how nice it would be if they put Derek into an institution where they could visit him a couple of times a year and then forget him, it indicated how dearly Slocum wanted to re-experience the old sense of the future, a future toward which one willingly goes. But these fantasies only emphasized the bitter reality.

I am not suggesting that what happened to Slocum and his family is a representative story. What my experience clearly suggests, however, is that what they thought about and felt would be found in the internal dialogues of members of families with retarded children. Our society approves of expressions of love toward our children, but not of hate or ambivalence. We are expected to give priority to our children's needs over our own needs, and to deny ourselves self-expression and self-fulfillment in order to insure that our children's need for untrammeled growth will be met. Some parents can follow society's dictates and contain the negative side of their ambivalence at no great cost. The negative side is there but it does not become unduly disruptive to self or others. Some parents follow society's dictates but at a high cost to their sense of well-being and family integration, and the Slocums are only one of many types who fall into this group. And then there are those parents (like Cynthia and Harold, and Keith's parents) who reject society's dictates, with massive disruptions to existing relationships. What is common to all of these parents, because of the way mental retardation is perceived in our society, is that they are confronted with the task of accommodating themselves to an altered future, an accommodation that, whatever its consequences and quality, is preceded by grief and the extension of the sense of isolation.

I have been concentrating on parental reaction for two reasons. The first is that they are coping with one of the most difficult experiences people in our society can have. The second reason is that it illuminates the enormous differences between the experience of the normal and the retarded young child. The gleeful, doting parents approach, touch, manipulate, and hug the normal infant, even though they may be concerned that they are too intrusive and may "spoil" the child, fearing that the child may come to think that the world exists only to fulfill his or her needs. The parents seize, rightly or wrongly, on any action that suggests that their child shows signs of precociousness. They know he is normal; they would like him to be supernormal. Rarely is one human being so aware of, so responsive to, so indulgent of, and so selfless toward another human being as a parent in the parent-infant relationship.

But what about the parents of a retarded infant? Preoccupied with their own altered needs, dimly sensing a future they never imagined, plagued with anxiety and frequently guilt and anger, searching the past for reasons and the present for hope, they cannot evade the knowledge that planning and hoping are frail reeds on which to restructure lives. They experience those too frequent, piercing reminders that by virtue of someone's coming into their lives, a good deal has gone out of it and they must bury treasured hopes and fantasies. Caught up in this swirl of personal despair, it is the rare parent who can respond unanxiously, spontaneously, and competently to the infant. When you are absorbed with yourself and your future, a limit is set on what you can be aware of and respond to in others. To give of yourself to someone else when you feel you need so much for yourself is extraordinarily difficult, if not impossible. Similarly, to give in order to secure someone else's future when your own personal future is in doubt is asking too much.

Matters are usually made worse by the professionals who communicate the fateful diagnosis to the parents. For one thing, they confuse communicating the diagnosis with being helpful. For another thing, they (usually) unwittingly discuss the infant more as if it were as thing than a human being (i.e., a damaged or incomplete object toward whom the usual parental response will not have productive consequences). The infant can become an object of fear or a strange puzzle that the parents cannot figure out alone. The parents have been given a diagnosis, but no guidelines or specific directions about how to think and act in the course ahead.

Earlier I stressed the significance of parental coping with an altered *personal* future. The difficulty of that deeply personal and private task is increased by parental inability to imagine what the child will be like in the future. Will the child walk, talk, laugh, respond, play, go to school? Will the child look different? The number of questions seems infinite, and they are asked and unanswered endlessly.

But behind these questions is an *assumption* that professionals too often have instilled in parents: *that the answers to the questions about the child's future will be determined exculsively or largely by the nature of the child's condition, and minimally or far less by the transactions between parents and child.* That is to say, the condition will unravel itself, and parents and others who participate in the child's rearing are more like bystanders watching a predetermined developmental unfolding. This of course, is conceptual nonsense and in flat contradiction to experience and research. But unfortunately, this has not prevented the acceptance of this unwarranted assumption in clinical diagnosis and action.

OPTIMISIM AND THE FUTURE

How do we account for the recurring interest in Itard's *Wild Boy of Aveyron*, a case study begun at the end of the Eighteenth Century and completed at the beginning of the Nineteenth Century? It has been a source of fascination and controversy, used for almost two centuries by different people to illustrate different points. In 1976, a new book was published by Harlan Lane on Itard's work with the "Wild Boy" Victor, bringing together for the first time new and old documents about the case. It is a book deserving careful reading and a long quotation:

> The story begins one day in 1797, in the fifth year of the new French Republic, when peasants in the region of Lacaune, in south central France, spied a naked boy fleeing through the woods called La Bassine. Curiosity aroused, they lay in wait on the following days and finally saw him again searching for acorns and roots. In 1798 he was sighted again by woodsmen and, despite violent resistance, taken to the village of Lacaune, where his arrival created a sensation. He was put on display several times in the public square, but the crowd's curiosity was quickly satisfied by the sight of the filthy mute urchin and, under relaxed surveillance, he was able to escape into the forest.
>
> Over the next fifteen months, the wild boy was seen from time to time in the fields on the edge of the forest, digging up potatoes and turnips, which he ate on the spot or occasionally carried off. Several lairs were found and attributed to him, including one with a bed of leaves and moss. Then, on July 25, 1799, three hunters spotted him in the same woods, gave chase, and succeeded in dislodging him from a tree. Tied up tight, he was led back to Lacaune and entrusted to the care of an old widow. This devoted guardian, one of her contemporaries recounts, dressed him in a sort of gown to hide his nakedness and offered him various foods, including raw and cooked meat, which he always refused. He did accept acorns, chestnuts, walnuts, and potatoes, always sniffing them before putting them in his mouth. When not eating or sleeping, he prowled from door to door and window to window seeking to escape. After eight days, he succeeded.
>
> This time the wild boy did not return to the forest. Climbing the nearby mountains he gained the broad plateau between Lacaune and Roqueceziere, in the department of Aveyron. Through the autumn, and into a particularly cold winter, he wandered over this elevated and sparsely populated region, entering occasionally into farmhouses where he was fed. When given potatoes, he threw them into the coals of the hearth, retrieving and eating them only a few minutes later. During the day, he was seen swimming and drinking in streams, climbing trees, running at great speed on all fours, digging for roots and bulbs in the fields; and, when the wind blew from the Midi, turning toward the sky he rendered up deep cries and great bursts of laughter. Finally, working his way down the mountain along the course of the Lavergne and Vernoubre rivers, he arrived on the outskirts of the village of Saint-Sernin. Encouraged perhaps by the treatment he had received from the farmers on the plateau, urged on perhaps by hunger, he approached the workshop of the dyer Vidal. It was seven o'clock in the morning, January 8, 1800. The boy slipped across the threshold into a new life, and into a new era in the education of man.

(pp. 6-7)

For our purposes we can do no better than to give a sample of Lane's succinct, moving, and personal account:

> The Luxembourg Gardens are an island of calm, of lawns, gravel paths, fountains, and statues, in the heart of left-bank Paris. On a summer's day in 1800, two young Frenchmen from the provinces met there for the first time and joined together their lives and futures. Although neither could have said so, each was engaged in a search whose success required the other.

71

The first young man was well but not elegantly dressed in a long coat, drawn in at the waist, with full lapels. His curly hair fell in locks over a slanting forehead; his aquiline nose extended the plane almost as far as his jutting chin. Tightly drawn wide lips and large, dark brown eyes completed the Mediterranean features, set off by a broad white collar that rose funnel-like from his frilly white shirt. Jean-Marc-Gaspard Itard was twenty-six and had just become a doctor. He had left the barren village at the foot of the French Alps where he was raised and had come to Paris in search of a place for himself in the new social order that had emerged from the chaos of the Revolution. Paris at this time was vibrant: painting, theater, music, and literature were flourishing, abetted by the glittering salons of the very rich, the rendezvous of the intellectual and social elite. Medicine was surging ahead; it had become possible to protect people against disease by giving them some of the disease itself, although no one really knew why. One of Itard's teachers, Philippe Pinel, had just written the first book on psychiatric diagnosis, and had dramatically ordered inmates of the city's insane asylums to be unchained. The first anthropological society was formed, while expeditions returned with the flora, fauna, and inhabitants of Africa, Indonesia, and the New World, to the delight and fascination of naturalists, anatomists, and, above all, philosophers. Itard had left the relative isolation of the provinces in search of this excitement of senses and mind, to share in it, even to contribute to it if he could. His alliance with the strange boy rocking back and forth in front of him would surely bring him public attention; it might admit him to the ranks of the great doctors and philosophers of his time, or it might destroy his career right at its beginning.

The boy was twelve or thirteen years old, but only four-and-a-half feet tall. Light-complexioned, his face was spotted with traces of smallpox and marked with several small scars, on his eyebrow, on his chin, on both cheeks. Like Itard, he had dark deep-set eyes, long eyelashes, chestnut brown hair, and a long pointed nose; unlike Itard, the boy's hair was straight, his chin receding, his face round and childlike. His head jutted forward on a long graceful neck, which was disfigured by a thick scar slashed across his voice box. He was clothed only in a loose-fitting gray robe resembling a nightshirt, belted with a large leather strap. The boy said nothing; he appeared to be deaf. He gazed distantly across the open spaces of the gardens, without focusing on Itard or, for that matter, on anything else. That same day, he had ended a grueling week-long journey. By order of the Minister of the Interior, Napoleon Bonaparte's brother, Lucien, the boy had come to Paris from a forest region in the province of Aveyron in southern France. This journey was the latest development in his search, which began a year before when he clambered out of the forests, worked his way across an elevated plateau in the bitterest winter in recent memory, and entered a farmhouse on the edge of a hamlet. He exchanged the freedom and isolation of his life in the forests of Aveyron, where he had run wild, for captivity and the company of men in society. He came without a name, so he was called the Wild Boy of Aveyron.

Perhaps Itard knew better than the savants of his time, who expected to see in the boy the incarnation of Rousseau's "noble savage," man in the pure state of nature; perhaps he did not. What he saw, he wrote later, was "a disgustingly dirty child affected with spasmodic movements, and often convulsions, who swayed back and forth ceaselessly like certain animals in a zoo, who bit and scratched those who opposed him, who showed no affection for those who took care of him; and who was, in short, indifferent to everything and attentive to nothing." The society of the eighteenth century had held both young men at bay, depriving the first of the best it had to offer, depriving the second of everything. Itard sought to master the ultimate skills of his culture — trained observation, persuasive language, social grace — the boy, their rudiments. So be it: they would help each other. Educating the boy would be a test of the new science of mental medicine and a proof of philosophy's new empiricist theory of knowledge. It would give still more justification for social reform by showing how utterly man depends on society for all that he is and can be. If the effort succeeded, the nineteenth century would give them their proper place, where the eighteenth had not.

Much more than a century later, nearly two, I sat in the Luxembourg Gardens and wondered about the two young men who had met there. Off to my left, the National Institute for Deaf-Mutes, where Itard had taken the wild boy to live and to learn. There, in his efforts to train him, Itard created a whole new approach to education, centered on the pupil, closely adapted to his developing needs and abilities, seconded by instructional devices — an approach we have accepted so thoroughly as our ideal that we scarcely imagine any other or credit anyone with its discovery. Behind me, the Sorbonne, where Itard had defended the possibility of educating the boy against the judgment of the great philosophers and doctors of the time, who contended that the boy was left in the wild because he was an idiot, not an idiot because he was left in the wild. Behind me, and farther north, the Academy of Medicine, where Itard read his historic reports on methods for teaching the deaf and the retarded to speak — methods he had developed with the wild boy. In front of me and to the south, the Hospital for Incurables, where Itard's student, Edouard Seguin, set out to prove that idiots were educable, contrary to unanimous medical opinion; where George Sumner came to see Itard's methods in action, bringing them back to America to start the education of the retarded there; where, finally, Maria Montessori came, to end by extending Itard's methods to the education of the normal preschool child as well as the handicapped.

Thinking of these places close at hand, where the drama of Dr. Itard and the wild boy took place, shaping the lives of countless children up through my own time, imagining the excitement of another time when men affirmed, "Yes, the deaf *can* speak, the retarded *can* learn," when they believed that the only sure limit to a child's knowledge is his society's ignorance, when they were convinced, as I am, of the perfectibility of man — thinking of these times and places one summer afternoon in the Luxembourg Gardens, I decided to begin my own search, to find Itard and the wild boy. I retraced their steps, gathering copies of letters and documents as I went. The town hall in Rodez and the regional archives for Aveyron, the boiler-room "archives" and library of the National Institute for the Deaf, the dusty attics of the Sorbonne and School of Medicine (with the priceless view of Paris rooftops accorded only to students and cleaning ladies), the opulent quarters of the National Archives and the Academy of Medicine, the corridors of the hospitals Bicetre and Val-de-Grace, a dozen other places but especially the cavernous hushed reading rooms of the National Library: these were my joyful haunts in every spare minute for two years.

Here is the outcome — a moving story about how a man and a boy helped each other in the search for knowledge, and how that search changed their lives and ours.

(pp. 3-6)

We shall not be concerned here with the more obvious points of interest in the Itard-Victor saga: how the whole affair was rooted in competing philosophies of the time; the enormous changes it represented in man's view of man; the fantastic degree of thought, planning, persistence, experimentation, and devotion that characterized the efforts of Itard and his helpers; and the final and wide discrepancy between the goals sought and attained and how the discrepancy was interpreted by competing theorists.

Victor never became "normal." But the difference in Victor before and after his encounters with Itard was vast indeed. Two points deserve emphasis. The first is the relationship between optimism and results. Put in another way: Itard did not see Victor as a victim of a "condition" (whatever its bodily nature) that doomed him in the future no less than in the past, but rather as a victim of a lack of normal social intercourse. If Victor could be enticed to participate in normal social relationships in an ambience of love, support and stimulation, his dormant capabilities would become manifest. From Itard's perspective there was a future for Victor, but that future depended on how Itard met the pedogogical problem: how to stimulate, motivate, sustain and build upon Victor's existing behavioral repertoire. *The challenge was Itard's!* If he failed, it would say as much about his inadequacies as Victor's limitations. What a contrast to a view of the future we see so frequently today in regard to Victor-like infants!

The second point deserving emphasis is a subtle one. Itard was not only a diagnostician, but he also participated in and supervised Victor's daily life. He not only gave advice, he implemented it. He *knew* Victor as few, if any, clinicians today know their child patients. Itard both structured and participated in Victor's social context. And if an approach or technique did not work, *he* tried another. Itard's optimism was grounded in a point of view that made it seem natural to persist in experiments and to be patient and loving. If Itard failed, it was a magnificent failure. He demonstrated what willing and total involvement can achieve when the odds against it seem overwhelmingly high, and that, in my opinion, is why his work will always be a chapter in the history of individual accomplishment. When we look at how parents of retarded infants and young children are "helped" by the diagnosticians and prescribers, we can begin to understand why a parent (like Slocum) may have raging anger toward those who help. How many of these diagnosticians/prescribers have been in the home to observe, advise and demonstrate? In my experience, the answer is none.

There are parents like Itard, but they do not write. For example, there was a youth named David who was carried in the arms of a man from a car to the institution in which he would spend the rest of his life. The distance from the door of the admissions building to the car was about twenty yards and it appeared as if the man were carrying a young but somewhat large grown child. But that apparent child was chronologically a young man with cerebral palsy involving all of his extremities. He seemed to be never at rest because of athetoid, purposeless, uncontrollable muscular action, and his speech, for all practical purposes, was unintelligible because when he tried to respond, the uncontrollable body movements became exacerbated. He was as handicapped a case of cerebral palsy as some of the staff had ever seen. His optimistic, supportive mother had recently died, his father had died when he was a young child, and there was no one at home to take care of him. Understandably, but wrongly, he seemed on initial impression to be severely retarded. There was, it was thought, no reason to evaluate him quickly, and he was placed in a building for the severely retarded.

Three weeks later the admitting psychologist met the staff aide in charge of that building and when he was asked how David was doing, the reply was: "He's a real smart fellow." The psychologist was skeptical and this must have shown in his facial expression, because the aide said: "Come on over and I'll prove it to you." When the visit was arranged, David was lying in the seat of the wheelchair, gnarled, in motion, saliva dripping from his mouth, becoming more of a stream when the psychologist approached with a routine greeting to which David seemed to want to make a reply. Quite a sight! The aide gave the psychologist a large checkerboard that had accompanied David to the institution. In each of the squares was a large letter of the alphabet. "Ask him a question requiring a one word answer, then run your finger slowly across the checkerboard and when David wants you to stop at the first letter of the answer he'll let you know, and you then do that for the second letter of the answer, and so on." David, it turned out, was a very smart young man!

How did these parents rear David? How did his mother, confronted with such a severely handicapped infant, manage to reach the child? There are many more questions, but there are no answers. His case record was unrevealing except that he had been diagnosed as mentally retarded and, therefore, eligible to be placed in an institution for retarded children. How smart David was is really not the issue, and it is indulging pedantry and nit-picking to make an issue of what label one should pin on him. The important questions are: why was this mother, Itard-like, optimistic? What permitted her to shape a future that few others would have allowed themselves to imagine? What kept *her* going?

CONCLUSION

In the past two decades there have been two major promising changes in attitudes which have taken place as a result of a variety of factors. The first of these factors is the rise and influence of parent groups seeking an increase in the quantity of community services enabling parents to keep their child at home. In earlier days, institutionalization as often as not was the reluctant choice of parents who saw no other option. The second and related factor was the public recognition of the scandalous conditions in institutions. Exposés became frequent fare in the mass media. These inhumane conditions were more characteristic of the public than the private institution — and institutions for the mentally retarded were by no means unique in their conditions — but a generalized deeply negative attitude toward all "total" institutions was aroused in people. These two factors converged to make it easier for parents of young retarded children to remain in the community. "Mentally retarded individuals can and should remain in their home and community" — this new societal attitude became a matter of public policy.

But this attitudinal change has added a new aspect to an old problem because as the child remains at home and is entered in one or more educational-community programs, the parents are faced again with an old question: who *in the community* will care for our child when we are gone? This question is given force as parents learn that satisfactory program options for the maturing retarded individuals hardly exist. In many communities they do not exist at all. Parents may be prepared to keep their child at home or in some community setting as long as they live, but at the same time, they know that living in the community is subject to risks and dangers, and they also believe that these risks and dangers would be less than in a state institution. The fact is that the risks and dangers are different, not that one set is ''better'' than the other. The point, however, is that we rather grossly mislead ourselves and dilute our effectiveness if we underestimate the centrality of concern for the future in the lives of parents of retarded individuals.

WORKS CITED

Becker, Ernest, *The Denial of Death*. New York: Free Press, 1973.

Blatt, B., and F. Kaplan. *Christmas in Purgatory*. Boston: Allyn & Bacon, 1966.

Carver, J.J. and N.E. Carver. *The Family of the Retarded Child*. Syracuse, NY: Syracuse University Press, 1972.

Eaton, J.W., and R.J. Weil. *Culture and Mental Disorders: A Comparative Study of the Hutterites and Other Populations*. Glencoe, IL: Free Press, 1955.

Grossman, F.K. *Brothers and Sisters of Retarded Children: An Exploratory Study*. Syracuse, NY: Syracuse University Press, 1972.

Heller, Joseph. *Catch-22*. New York: Simon and Schuster, 1961.

_____. *Something Happened*. New York: Knopf, 1974.

Itard, Jean-Marc-Gaspard. *Wild Boy of Aveyron*. 1801; rpt. Englewood Cliffs, NJ: Prentice-Hall, 1962.

Lane, Harlan. *Wild Boy of Aveyron*. Cambridge: Harvard Univ. Press, 1976.

Sarason, S., and J. Doris. *Educational Handicap, Public Policy and Social History: A Broadened Perspective on Mental Retardation*. New York: Free Press, 1979.

STEREOTYPES AND CAPTAIN HOOK
by Lee Bailey

The concept of stereotype widely used in the social sciences was adopted from the journalist Walter Lippmann. In his *Public Opinion* (1922) he shows how simplified fictions, models or maps fill in the gaps of the unknown. Guiding selective perception and judgment, maintaining blind spots and socio-political codes, stereotypes reflect conclusions seeking evidence, judgments seeking confirmation, for:

> The pattern of stereotypes at the center of our codes largely determines what group of facts we shall see, and in what light we shall see them.

Far from neutral, these visions reveal value-laden defenses of personal and social position, guarantees of self-respect and rights. Like Aristotle's postulate that those meant to be slaves *are* those who are slaves, stereotypes express ways of seeing. Like a doorman at a masquerade who rejects inappropriate costumes, a stereotype prejudges the world according to expectations. Lippmann saw after World War I that:

> With the stereotype of 'progress' before their eyes, Americans have in the mass seen little that did not accord with that progress.

He agreed with Marx that we see through a class darkly.

Lippmann was influenced on this point by William James, who taught him that:

> *the only things which we commonly see are those which we preperceive...*which have been labeled for us ... If we lost our stock of labels we should be intellectually lost in the midst of the world.

The concept of a necessary ideational preparation in all understanding was not original to Lippmann, but he effectively applied it to the problem of stereotypes.

If stereotypes reveal the way we define first, and then see, the task of discrediting stereotypes of disability requires a clear understanding of the *source* of stereotypes. Lippmann acknowledges his debt to Freud's demonstrations of the importance of dream and fantasy in discovering the unconscious roots of rationalization and stereotype. But he does not recognize the mythic, archetypal elements in stereotypes: those archaic, persistent, imaginal responses to the permanent aspects of the human situation, whether love, death, family or disability.

Archetypal images have been understood as universals since Plato's theory of *eidolon,* and have been given a new basis in C. G. Jung's understanding of the collective unconscious. But Leslie Fiedler has come closest to recognizing the archetypal elements in images of disability. In his book *Freaks* (1978) he sees that stereotyped responses to disability are rooted in "primordial fears" of "scale, sexuality, or status as more than beasts and our tenuous individuality." In the fearful, fascinated response to small people, giants, hermaphroditic people, *l'enfant sauvage* and siamese twins, he discloses not personal, learned fantasies, but deep-rooted, ageless *memoria.* He recognizes that, like a traditional belief about dwarves, stereotypes of disability are "old as soon as [they] are born."

No analysis of the roots of disability stereotypes can be complete without recognition of these primordial, archetypal responses, for they provide the necessary images of the meaning of events. The power of the very myths, maps and models Lippmann describes as unconscious determinants of perception and judgment is better understood to the extent that the primordial element is recognized. This is not to imply that education cannot modify primordial images, but that the presuppositions carried in archaic images *are* "education," unless they can be critically re-imagined.

The recognition of the primordial force of disability stereotypes is a two-edged sword. On one side the *ageless,* immemorial quality of fears of disability seems to make them impermeable, resistant to change and re-education. Not so. Archetypal responses to primordial events, whether love, death, family or disability, are innumerable and need not be oppressive. On the other side of the sword, these primordial responses to disability are only *fantasies*—wispy myths which should be the easiest errors to discredit. Yet the stubborn defensiveness of stereotypical fantasies shows how significantly fantasies are involved in perception, thought and judgment. If stereotypes are age-old because they are archetypal and powerful because they are primordial, they are also subject to change because they are only fantasies. This is the irony of stereotypes — they are stubborn and powerful because primordial and archetypal, yet they are *only* fantasies.

The task of the iconoclast then, is both to recognize the powerful archaic forces at work in images of disability and to understand their fundamentally fantastic nature. For it is in hearing the archaic stories behind the fantasies that we can begin to differentiate between image and individual, between a collective fantasy and a person who happens to have a disability. This differentiation is the key to overcoming stereotypical behavior. But it demands an eye for both the archaic and the imaginal.

In philosophy this difficulty is at work in the problem of the relations between universals and particulars. A stereotype is a universal image which has become a cliché: the cripple, the retard or the freak— a stock response to certain particulars. Such an error is a case of the fallacy of misplaced concreteness, of an inappropriate reduction of a universal, archetypal fantasy to a particular individual. Lippmann is right in seeing how stereotypes uncover conclusions seeking evidence, or fantasies seeking examples. And Fiedler is right in seeing the archetypal, primordial roots of stereotypes. Both insights need each other. And they both gain from the awareness of the fantastic quality of sterotypical images, from the vision of the shadows behind the literal, the archaic universals lurking about judgments of particulars. For losing the sense of the fantastic in the midst of the "realistic" is to lose contact with a fundamental key to overcoming stereotypical behavior. A good example of such a fantastic image with stereotypical overtones is Captain Hook, a disabled villain whose mythic background discloses archaic, primordial depth.

CAPTAIN HOOK

In the most chilling lines in J.M. Barrie's *Peter Pan* (1904), the vile Captain Hook's pirate mates sing:

Avast, belay, when I appear
By fear they're overtook.
Nought's left upon your bones when you
Have shaken claws with Hook!

The hook is this fantasy character's outstanding image, and it is an instrument of ruthless destruction. If we let this fantasy speak as a symbolic expression of a primordial experience, the hook has no direct correlation to a specific disability, but evokes the generic cut-off-ness inherent in human existence.

Peter Pan's wicked enemy was Blackbeard's bo'sun, "the worst of them all." He was "cadaverous and blackavized," he treated his men like dogs, and his eyes had a "profound melancholy, save when he was plunging his hook into you, at which time two red spots appeared in them and lit them horribly." He was a disabled, death-dealing scoundrel, and "undoubtedly the grimmest part of him was his iron claw."

Hook's cadaverous wickedness reflects the primeval horror of being cut off, crippled in the broadest sense of being soft vulnerable fragments of flesh existing for a fleeting moment in a vast cosmos. A pirate in Hook's crew clumsily lurches against Hook, ruffling his lace collar, and:

the hook shoots forth, there is a tearing sound and one screech, then the body is kicked aside, and the pirates pass on. [Hook] has not even taken the cigar from his mouth.

The hook rips, maiming and killing, crippling and disfiguring arbitrarily and thoughtlessly. Instrument of this fearful, fateful force, the hook evokes the terror of a brush with a dark, brooding, violent power bringing loss, bitterness and melancholy: Mister Death.

The hand replaced by a hook was cut off by Peter Pan and flung to the crocodile which now relentlessly pursues Hook:

[Hook] lowered his voice. 'It liked my arm so much, Smee, that is has followed me ever since, from sea to sea, and from land to land, licking its lips for the rest of me... I want Peter Pan, who first gave the brute its taste for me...Smee,' he said huskily, 'that crocodile would have had me before this, but by a lucky chance it swallowed a clock which goes tick inside it, and so before it can reach me I hear the tick and bolt.' He laughed, but in a hollow way.

Hook is never alone. He is attached to a beast, the crocodile pursuing him with a clock in its belly. The clock-monster carries the inevitability of time's ravages. It is a part of Hook: the devouring, monstrous, chronological aspect of that terrible force which cuts off.

Certainly one of Hook's literary predecessors is Cap'n Ahab, whose missing leg was snatched by the great whale in Herman Melville's *Moby Dick* (1851). Like Hook, Ahab was thereafter fired with the lust for revenge. The greatest of Hook's historical predecessors, the European pirates, yearned not for such terrible images, but rather for a semblance of respectability; some even commissioned portraits of themselves as aristocrats. But literary tradition is the tradition of fantasy, so fictional pirates such as Hook and Long John Silver, in Stevenson's *Treasure Island* (1883), are frequently granted eyepatches, peg legs and hooks.

Hook wants nothing more than his revenge; his conflict with Peter Pan is the mainspring of the plot. And what is Peter Pan's mythic background? Barrie incorporated into Peter Pan motifs from Celtic fairy lore such as fairy levitation and the journey to fairyland. But his namesake is the ancient Greek god Pan, whose name means "feeder" and "everywhere" or "all." Pan unconceals the amorous force which makes the flocks fertile, which gives new life and fresh vitality in contrast with the villain and his clock-monster. Eternally new, Peter wants to never grow up:

'I don't want ever to be a man,' [Peter] said with a passion, 'I want always to be a little boy and to have fun. So I ran away from Kensington Gardens and lived a long time among the fairies.'

Peter embodies the pulsing energies of growth, the freedom of youthful vision, imagination and play. He is an image of Eternal Youth, the opposite of Mister Death, the one who cuts off, Captain Hook. This scoundrel, as aging and death, disability and fateful limit, hates children — that is, youth and renewal, vitality and growth. The fantasy of Hook's hatred for Pan discloses the conflict between eternal cutting-off and eternal renewal. The old man hates and kills new life, but youthful forces retaliate by cutting off the old man's power to destroy as well, for Peter cut off the pirate's hand in the beginning. The two figures, hero and villain, are opposites and extremes, but they are inseparably connected. Just as Father Time traditionally appears at the end of the old year along with the Infant signifying the new year, beginning and ending are simultaneous, occuring constantly.

Hook and Pan are versions of a larger archetypal pattern which the archetypal psychologist James Hillman has called *Senex* and *Puer* (old man and youth). He has shown the phenomenology of this primordial pattern to be characterized by the contrast between *Senex* images of old age, decline, disability, decay, helplessness, hopelessness and death, and *Puer* images of youth, progress, health, vitality, optimism and new life. As archetypal images, these characteristics cannot be restricted to one stage of life or to any one particular person. The polarity is a primordial image present universally as archaic, ageless experiences, as ground on which all stand, presences in which all participate.

KRONOS-SATURN MYTHOLOGY

Far back into the mists of Europe's past, far from the English world of fairies and pirates, we hear the echo of same story; we meet Captain Hook's mythic ancestor, the Greek god Kronos, a vengeful character who cuts with a hooked blade. The earliest surviving account of him casts the story as a violent conflict over the succession of power from father to son. Kronos, having castrated his father Uranos with a sickle, in turn became the father of the Olympian gods. Learning of his eventual overthrow by his own children, he swallowed them all except Zeus, who finally defeated him and took over rule of the cosmos. The Greek mythographer Hesiod describes Kronos' violent deed:

> Gaia's [Earth's] youngest-born was devious - division Kronos, most terrible of her children; and he hated his strong father [Uranos -Sky]... Presently creating the element of gray flint, [Gaia] made of it a great sickle,... [Kronos] reached with his left hand and seized [Uranos], and holding in his right hand the enormous sickle with its long blade edged like teeth, he swung it sharply, and lopped off the member of his own father.

But later, when Kronos became a father himself:

> as each of [his] children came from the womb of its mother, to her knees, great Kronos swallowed it down with the intention that no other of the proud children of the line of Uranos should ever hold the king's position among the immortals.

Like Captain Hook, Kronos hates children, attempts to destroy them and cuts with a hooked blade. He hated his own father, but when he became a father, he hated his own children and wanted to prevent them from attaining his own power. As images of primordial universals rather than as history, characters such as Kronos can play both parts in the story: youth and old man, Puer and Senex.

Kronos' story is the myth of the aging, decline and end of one generation as it is 'cut off' by the vital energies of a new generation. This archetypal motif lends itself to an emphasis on the sickle, the hooked blade which in agriculture cuts off the ripe grain. Kronos in this aspect is an image of the universal, seasonal round of generations.

As Kronos' story developed through amplification, the darker, shadowy side was soon emphasized. His phenomena were imagined for example, as-if a gloomy, solitary dethroned god were exiled below the earth. Hellenistic mythographers let Kronos' myth be expressed by the planet observed to be the slowest in its revolution, and so imagined as most distant and cold. The Romans named the god and this planet Saturn.

Over the subsequent centuries Saturn gathered about him fantasies of holding the fate of all fathers and old men, of time, celibacy, childlessness, widowhood, child exposure, orphanhood, violence, hidden malice, sadness, worry, misused beggars, captivity, and dethronement. In the pattern of the seven ages of man, Saturn was imagined last, as the saddest phase of life, old age and its loneliness, its physical and mental decay.

In the classic *Saturn and Melancholy* (1964) Klibansky, Panofsky and Saxl observe that "Saturn in particular, became in later medieval art more and more the leader and representative of the poor and the oppressed;" he became identified with beggars, prisoners, criminals and *cripples*. By the Renaissance, a long tradition had developed associations with physical illness and most outstanding, with Melancholy, what we today call despair or depression.

Recognized as universals, as archetypal, primordial images, these depressing fantasies of decay and disability cannot be identified with any particular individual. Saturn was not imagined as we would imagine a villain in a work of fiction, but as a transcendent yet immanent fateful factor in life, as a ground on which all stand, a presence in which all participate. No individual person can be identified with such a power, whether hero or villain, morally pure or disabled. Each individual participates in innumerable primordial patterns, each of which may be known as an idea, a model, a fantasy or a god.

KRONOS-SATURN ICONOGRAPHY

The record of Kronos-Saturn in visual art brings us closer to Captain Hook by following the traces of the identifying image of his sickle into Renaissance art. Kronos appears rarely in Ancient Greek art, and then only enthroned or with his wife Rhea. But Hellenistic and Roman art is more revealing (see Appendix B). A wall painting that survived Pompeii's volcanic burial (Illus. 1) sets forth the standard iconographic motif identifying Kronos-Saturn: the sickle. This stern-eyed god holds the instrument of cutting-off the seeds of life with his robe over his head, perhaps as a gesture of mourning. A Renaissance copy of a calendar of 354 repeats this iconography, without the stern countenance (Illus. 4). A Macedonian coin (Illus. 2) pictures the nude Kronos seated on a rock throne, holding the identifying sickle. Illustration 3 is a coin from Tarsus whose figure is either Kronos or Perseus (who decapitated the Gorgon Medusa) with a sickle-sword used for tree pruning. In an Eleventh century painting (Illus. 5) Saturn holds a scythe, the large-scale sickle which dominates modern images of Saturn as the Grim Reaper or Father Time. The small sickle survives as Captain Hook's claw.

Klibansky and Panofsky have collected a number of Renaissance images of Saturn. In a Sixteenth Century drawing of Saturn and his children (Illus. 6), a fully amplified visual iconography of Saturn equips him with a chariot on high pulled by the Dragon of Time. He carries with him his opposite the Child, corresponding to the later Peter Pan. Saturn's manifestations in daily life are indicated in the lower portion of the print, and the text associates him with the heavy metal lead (*plumbo*). The classical anatomy of Illus. 2 appears again here, and the astrological signs in the upper corners indicate his identification with the planet, which corresponds to the image of flying. A Paris manuscript, the *Epistle of Othea* (Illus. 7) clearly expresses the cosmological image of Saturn, seated on the heavenly spheres, sickle in hand, reaching towards his children seated below. The gruesome image of Saturn devouring children, dominant in Hesiod's account, was often represented visually in Renaissance drawings (Illus. 8, 9, 10, 11, 12, 13 and 17). This motif parallels Captain Hook's pursuit of Peter Pan and the lost boys.

The Dragon of Time (Illus. 8 and 14) who wraps himself around Saturn's scythe-scepter or pulls his chariot (Illus. 6) corresponds to Captain Hook's devouring crocodile - with - clock. They evoke the fearful, monstrous quality of the Kronos phenomenon of cutting-off, as some of disability's fearful fantasy creatures.

In 1581 Saturn with a scythe appears in an astrological text (Illus. 9) riding the clouds and violently devouring a child, while a feminine *Conscientia* points out the heavenly vision to an old man with an hourglass at his feet. A Rimini Saturn with flowing drapery (Illus. 10) grasps his sickle while the Child struggles desperately to escape his fate. A Northern European drawing of Saturn devouring the Child (Illus. 11) incorporates the typical scythe, a dragon, a serpent and the children of Saturn, but also the unusually frank image of a youth castrating the god. This stark image of Hesiod's myth reflects both sides of the violent conflict of youth and age: the Father devouring the Child and the Child cutting off the Father's generative capacity. The star above, the glimmering planet Saturn, also doubles as a prudent fig-leaf (Illus. 16 and 20).

The violent hatred and fear in Illus. 12, combined with the interest in classical anatomy, express the contrast between life's energies and death's ravages. The contrasted energy and corpse-like anatomy of Saturn as *Melancholia* (Illus. 13) evoke a shocking quality unknown in surviving images of Saturn in Antiquity. The *Melancholia* of Saturn here is not a fantasy peripheral to any imagined "objective" reality but is an pervasive as death itself, as the hangman's tree below announces.

In the Fourteenth Century text *Ovid Moralisé* (Illus. 14), Saturn is enthroned holding the Child and scythe with the entwined Dragon of Time. Unlike the attendants, Saturn and the Child have eye contact with the man from the depths, the underworld god. The unrecognized ancestor of Captain Hook's instrument of terror is like the small sickle held by a flying "Time cutting the wings of Cupid" from a 1567 text (Illus. 15). The wings on both Time and Cupid place them in the Never-Never Land of fantasy images that is everywhere. And the fantasy of Time attempting to trim Cupid's wings corresponds to Hook's yearning to stop Pan's flightly childishness and vitality.

To complete the iconography of the sickle-bearer as the one who cuts off, we find several images of Saturn with the crutch. A book of the Zodiac from 1470 (Illus. 16) illustrates the old man gazing into the distance with his toothed sickle, star-fig-leaf and a crutch. In three works entitled "The Triumph of Time," Saturn is winged, leans on a crutch and rides a processional cart pulled by reindeer (Illus. 17, 18 and 19). The first, an illustrations in a Petrarch text, (Illus. 17), gives Saturn a crutch despite a youthful body, and an aged head devouring the Child. The second, a painting in Fiesole (Illus. 18), shows him hunchbacked on crutches, holding an hourglass, supported below by winged youths. The third, another Petrarch illustration (Illus. 19), emphasizes Saturn's weary eyes as he stoops over his crutches, surrounded by ghostly skull-like faces in a barren landscape. A 1470 block print (Illus. 20) adds to the sickle, the crutch and the astrological images a peg-leg, worn by the sour-faced man with a crutch in the right foreground. The stress on daily life here speaks of Saturn as present in both the sowing and reaping of agricultural cycles and the cutting off of the stocks, the peg-leg, the chopping block and the hangman's noose.

STEREOTYPE AND HOOK

Stereotypes are not a things "out there" and cannot be changed as if "external." Stereotypes reveal ways of seeing, ways of reading archetypal images as clichés, as uncritical and unimaginative ways of interpreting primordial images. To awaken conventional consciousness from its stereotyping slumber, iconoclastic criticism can give the gift of a gentle kiss of imagination. To be able to move out of the defensive bastion of conventional myths, one must be able to re-imagine, not de-imagine, for imaginal models and maps are essential to understanding. The difference between stubborn stereotypical thought and critical imagination is the awareness that stereotypes are only fantasies. But both are powerful archetypal images which guide perception and judgment. And as universals, they cannot be reduced to the confines of a particular person or event. Such primordial images disclose the ground on which existence is made possible, not mere particulars. Captain Hook is about everyone and no one; he is everywhere and nowhere.

To re-imagine the terror of experiencing that:

Naught's left upon your bones when you
Have shaken claws with Hook

is to step back from the narrow everydayness of things and to see the visions, hear the echoes from the primeval forest. To become more comfortable with both the Child and the Hook, Puer and Senex, is to discover the impossibility of stereotypically reducing such vast forces to the narrow confines of one person. Disability prejudice, re-imagined as a false concretization of an archetypal image in which all participate, can be countered imaginally as well as politically.

WORKS CITED

Barrie, J.M. *Peter Pan*. NY: Scribner's 1904, pp. 62-81.

Fiedler, Leslie. *Freaks: Myths and Images of the Secret Self*. NY: Simon and Schuster, 1978, pp. 24, 45.

Harding, John. "Stereotypes." *Encyclopedia of Social Sciences*. NY: Macmillan, 1968. 15:259-262.

Hesiod. *Theogony, Works and Days*. Trans. R. Lattimore. Ann Arbor: Univ. Michigan Pr., 1970. *Theogony* 155, 459.

Hillman, James. "The Negative Senex and a Renaissance Solution." *Spring* 1975. Includes bibliography of his Senex articles.

_____, ed. *Puer Papers*. Dallas, TX: Spring Pub., 1979.

James, William. *The Principles of Psychology*. 1890; rpt. NY: Dover, 1950. I:444.

Jung, Carl G. *The Collected Works of C.G. Jung*. ed. William McGuire. Trans. R.F.C. Hull. 20 Vols. Princeton: Bollingen, 1953-1978.

Klibansky, Raymond, Erwin Panofsky and Fritz Saxl. *Saturn and Melancholy*. NY: Basic Bks, 1964. Part II, Chapters 1 and 2. Illustrations 10, 31, 36, 46, 47, 48, 49, 52, 53.

Lippmann, Walter. "Stereotypes." *Public Opinion*. NY: Macmillan, 1930. pp. 79-156, esp. 85, 110, 125.

Mayer, Maximillian. "Kronos." In *Ausführliches Lexicon der Griechischen und Römischen Mythologie*. ed. Wilhelm Roscher. Leipzig: Teubner, 1890. II (1):1452-1573 and illustrations 6 and 8.

Melville, Herman. *Moby Dick*. 1851; rpt. NY: Abrams, 1976.

Panofsky, Erwin. "Father Time." *Studies in Iconology*. 1939; rpt. NY: Harper and Row (Icon), 1962. Plates xxiii, no. 39; xxiii, no. 40; xxiv, no. 45; xxv, no. 47; xxviii, no. 52; xxx, no. 55; xxxi, no. 56; xxxi, no. 57.

Roscher, Wilhelm, ed., *Ausführliches Lexicon der Griechischen und Romischen Mythologie*. Leipzig: Teubner, 1890. II (1):1452-1573 and illustrations 6 and 8.

Stevenson, Robert Louis. *Treasure Island*. 1883; rpt. NY: Macmillan, 1963.

Illustrations for
"Images of Disability in Art"

Fig. 1. John Millais (1829-1896), *The Blind Girl* (1856), by Courtesy of Birmingham (England) Museums and Art Gallery.

Fig. 2. Domenico Ghirlandaio (1449-1494), *Old Man and a Boy*, Musée du Louvre, Cliché des Musées Nationaux-Paris.

Fig. 3. Jusepe Ribera (1591-1652), *The Club-Footed Boy*
(1642), Musée du Louvre, Paris.

Fig. 4. Diego Velazquez (d. 1660), *Don Sebastian de Morra,*
Museo del Prado, Madrid.

Fig. 5. Rembrandt van Rijn (1606-1669), *Rembrandt's Mother,*
Rijksmuseum, Amsterdam.

Fig. 6. Rembrandt van Rijn (1606-1669),
Self-Portrait, Copyright the
Frick Collection, New York.

Fig. 7. Rembrandt van Rijn (1601-1669),
Old Man Praying, Cleveland Museum
of Art (67.16), Leonard C.
Hanna Jr. Bequest.

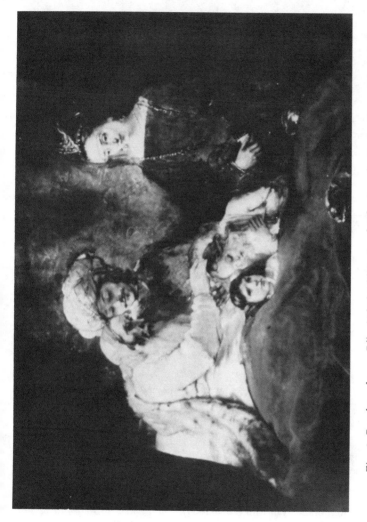

Fig. 8. Rembrandt van Rijn (1606-1669), *Jacob Blessing the Sons of Joseph* (1656), Staatliche Kunstsammlungen, Kassel (West Germany).

93

Fig. 9. Rembrandt van Rijn (1606-1669), *The Return of the Prodigal Son* (c. 1666), State Hermitage Museum, Leningrad.

Fig. 10. Rembrandt van Rijn (1606-1669), *Simeon and the Infant Christ,* National Museum, Stockholm.

Fig. 11. Pieter Brueghel the Elder (c. 1525-1569), *The Blind Leading the Blind* (1568), National Museum, Naples.

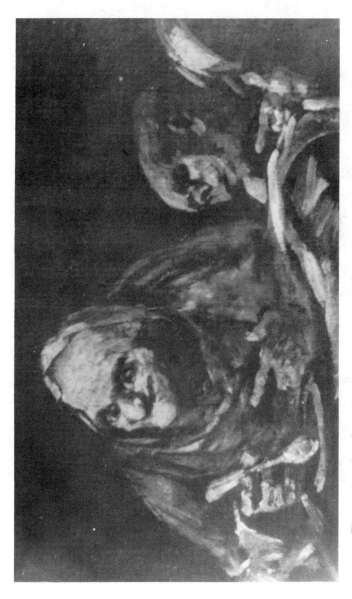

Fig. 12. Francisco de Goya (1746-1828), *Two Old Men Eating Porridge (Quinta del Sordo)*, (c. 1820), Museo del Prado, Madrid.

Fig. 13. Theodore Gericault (1791-1824), *A Madwoman (La Maraîchère)* (1823), Musée des Beaux-Arts, Lyon.

Fig. 14. Pablo Picasso (1881-1973), *The Blind Man's Meal,* The Metropolitan Museum of Art, New York, Gift of Mr. and Mrs. Ira Haupt, 1950.

Fig. 15. Pablo Picasso (1881-1973), *The Old Guitarist* (1903), The Art Institute of Chicago.

Fig. 16. Pablo Picasso (1881-1973), *The Dwarf Dancer* (1901), Museo Picasso de Barcelona.

© S.P.A.D.E.M., Paris/V.A.G.A., New York

Fig. 17. Pablo Picasso (1881-1973), *The Painter and Model* (1963), Courtesy of Sidney Janis Gallery, New York.

Fig. 18. Pablo Picasso (1881-1973), *The Family*
(India Ink on Linoleum Print).
Collection of Maximilian Schell, Munich.

Fig. 19. Rembrandt van Rijn (1606-1669), *Family Group*,
Herzog Anton Ulrich Museum, Braunschweig
(Brunswick, West Germany).

Fig. 20. Francisco de Goya (1746-1828), *Milkmaid of Bordeaux* (1827), Museo del Prado, Madrid.

Appendix B
Illustrations of Saturn for "Stereotypes and Captain Hook"

Illus. 1. Saturn, Pompeii, Casa dei
Dioscuri, Naples.
(Klibanski, Illus. 10.)

Illus. 2. Macedonian
Copper, Hellenistic.
(Roscher, "Kronos" Fig. 6).

Illus. 3. Tarsos Coin.
(Roscher, "Kronos"
Fig. 8).

105

Illus. 4. Saturn. Calendar of
354, Italian, after 15th
Century, Biblioteca
Vaticana. (Panofsky,
pl.XXIII, no. 39).

Illus. 5. Rabanus Maurus,
De Universo, c.1023,
Monte Cassino.
(Panofsky, pl. XXII,
no.40).

Saturnus in curru à Draconibus vectus, vel infantem falce
minitatur: Capricornum et Aquarium percurrit: Occidentem
possidet: Magis et sagis, fodinis et plumbo præest.

Illus. 6. Henri Leroy, *Saturn and his Children*, 16th Century.
(Klibanski, Illus. 53).

Illus. 7. Christine de Pisan,
Epitre d'Othea. (Klibanski, Illus. 36).

*Illus. 8. Saturn Enthroned with
Scythe,* 14th Century, Biblioteca
Vaticana. (Panofsky, pl.XXIV.
no. 45).

Illus. 9. Gerard de Jode, *Saturn devouring a child, Septem Planetae.*
(Klibanski, Illus. 48).

Illus. 10. Studio of Agnostini di Duccio, *Saturn,*
1554-55, Rimini, Tempio Malatestiano.
(Klibanski, Illus. 49).

Illus. 11. The castration of Saturn, 15th Century, Dresden, Kupferstichkabinett. (Klibanski, Illus. 4).

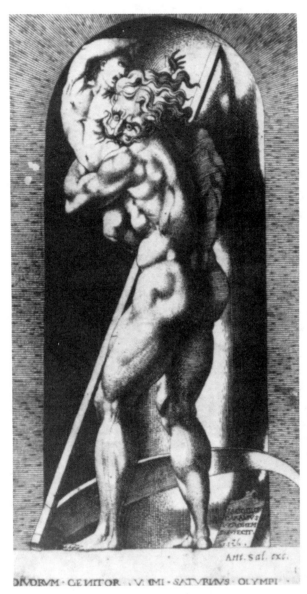

DIVORVM · GENITOR · V: (MI · SATVRNVS · OLYMPI ·

Illus. 12. Jacopo Caraglio, *Divorum Genitor - Saturn,*
1526. (Panofsky, pl.XXV, no. 47).

Illus. 13. Marten van Heemskerck, *Saturn and his Children,* 16th Century.
(Klibanski, Illus. 52).

Illus. 14. Saturn with the Dragon of Time, *Ovid Moralisé,* 14th Century, Bibliothèque Nationale, Paris. (Klibanski, Illus. 46).

Illus. 15. Time Cutting the Wings of Cupid, Otho Venius, *Les Emblems de l'Amour Humain,* 1567, Brussels. (Panofsky, pl. XXXI, no. 57).

Illus. 16. Saturn and his Zodiacal Signs, Vom den VII Zeichen des Gestirns, 1470, Zürich, Zentral Bibliothek. (Klibanski, Illus. 31).

Illus. 17. The Triumph of Time, Petrarch, 1560, Venice.
(Panofsky, pl.XXXI, no. 56).

Illus. 18. Jacopo del Sellaio (?) *The Triumph of Time*, Fiesole, Oratorio S.Ansano. (Panofsky, pl. XXX, no. 55).

Illus. 19. The Triumph of Time, Petrarch, 1493, Venice.
(Panofsky, pl. XXVIII, no. 52).

Illus. 20. Saturn and his Children, Blockbook, 1470, probably German copy of Netherlandish original. (Klibanski, Illus. 38).

INDEX